The Diary of A Rideshare Driver

THE DIARY
OF A
RIDESHARE
DRIVER

VASNA NOZARI

A BOOK BY:

Vasna Nozari

EDIT AND ADVISING:

Elham Samsani

Lee Barnathan

Pasha Lesan Pezeshki

Jasmin Pabua

CARTOONS AND GRAPHICS:

Ahmad Arabani

Mehrad Yousefi

Somaye Ezami

Vasna Nozari

COVER DESIGN AND PHOTOS:

Vasna Nozari

ReadersMagnet, LLC
10620 Treena Street, Suite 230 | San Diego, California, 92131 USA
1.619. 354. 2643 | www.readersmagnet.com

CONTENTS

In the name of GOD.

INTRODUCTION

Hello! This is me, a rideshare driver who loves to have a funny cartoon character and this book is about fun, adventure, and money. Enjoy it!

As you can see in the next picture, this cartoon comes from my real photo that I use for both of my rideshare profiles.

This book is the result of interesting adventures and it's not just about simple rideshare trips but it's also a journey through life.

I am writing this book as a rideshare driver-author. A driver who has something to share: the secret to being happy, to enjoying the job and a way to making more money than you can imagine. You will be wondering what's going on while reading these funny bits of nonsense, but in the end, it will actually make a lot of sense. I do small things that earned me tips that made me earn more than the actual trip**. This book is a collection of funny and sometimes strange, but real stories. These anecdotes are sometimes social, cultural, economic, even political, but are always thought-provoking. They are snippets of my experiences as a rideshare driver, the crazy adventures of a weird person who loves being a cartoon character with a funny mustache. Enjoy!

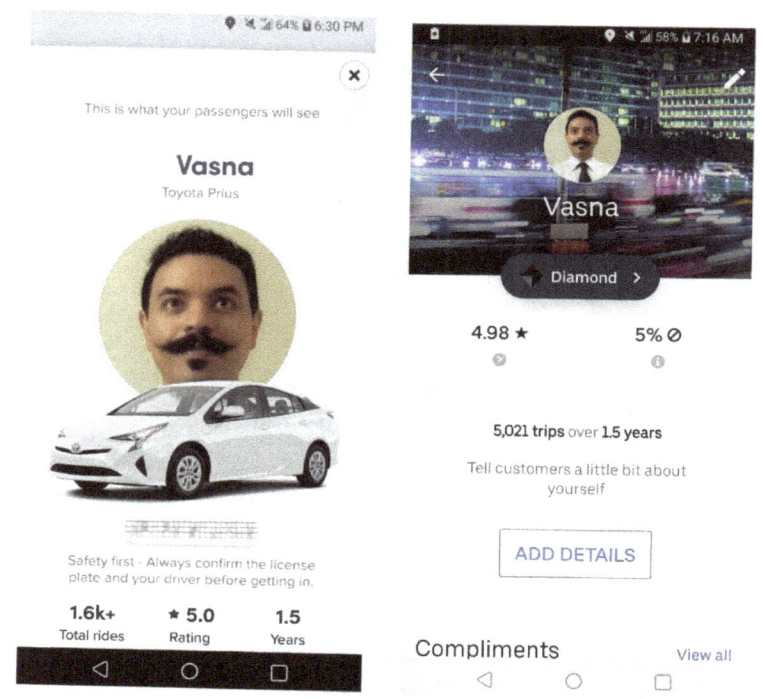

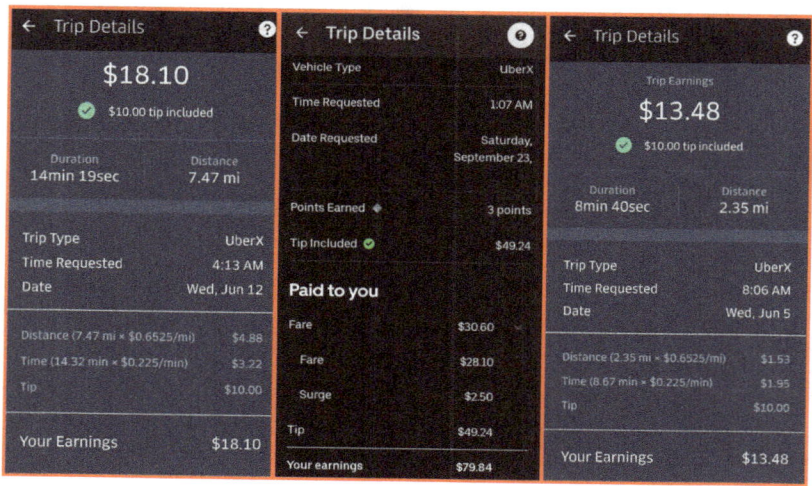

---

*   When I say "increasing the tip," I don't mean a couple of bucks more which is not that big a deal. Imagine being able to double your income! Look at the picture. What is the secret that can make a passenger who would only be in your car for 8 minutes decide to tip you more than 300% of the original fare?

CHAPTER I

Who Am I?!

When I was a kid, I was very proper and polite, a good kid without any signs of hyperactivity. Hmmm… honestly…I mean not that much hyperactivity. Maybe just a little! Indeed, I was always a little curious if I could make my imagination come alive in any situation. I was a good kid, believe me, I was just a little different!

Sir, have you ever seen lights come out from somebody's eyes?

Even until my teenage years, I was still a little different. My head literally grew faster than my body.

During my education time, I studied animal science, then movie directing, photography, and even a master's degree in International Marketing Management. I took more than ten certification courses because I like to read different subjects, no matter if I could use it or not.

Today, people say I'm a good photographer. I actually don't consider myself a photographer. I've only done it to pay bills since immigrating to the United States. Up to this point in my life, I have worked in so many different jobs, the variety is unbelievable. You may not even guess some of those!

I have been an advertising director, creative ideas man, product photographer, photo editor, video editor, screenplay writer, studio manager — the list can go on and even extend to me working in agriculture and on a university sheep farm!

Not convinced yet that I love doing odd things? Okaaaay...here's another surprise! For a while, I was in Alaska photographing wild bears, also doing a difficult and dangerous fishing job on the side. I decided I would start making a photobook from that. It hasn't been published yet, but I'm happy to have that experience and ...

Finally, I designed a cartoon and started my adventure as a rideshare driver. A rideshare driver with a funny mustache!

*　　*　　*

To know how this book was formed, again let's go back a little to my childhood age. I remember when I was a little boy, I loved reading "Father and Son" by German cartoonist Erich Ohser, which were for children...

... and I was reading the series "The Adventures of Tintin" by Belgian cartoonist Georges Remi, which probably was intended for an older audience.

Also, I eagerly read the books of Aziz Nesin, the Turkish satirist and militant secularist novelist who had written many critical comic short stories. These books were not for children!

MEMOIRS OF AN EXILE

AZIZ NESIN

Autobiography - Satire

And finally, I was reading the books of Persian satirist novelist Iraj Pezeshkzad. These books were not for kids at all!

Iraj Pezeshkzad

The point is I read all those books at the same age. I was a bookworm — a little weird bookworm! Still, this book is inspired by the works of those authors mentioned above.

Although I have some experience writing screenplays, I don't know enough about writing in English. So, this book is not going to be any great literary work written so I could receive literary awards or attract an audience by the power of beautiful literary sentences.

The main purpose of this book is to do my share of serving in life! Sharing some experiences so the reader might come away feeling good, giving economic ideas to drivers or small-business owners. I also have a dream to make enough money and I plan to donate the proceeds of this book, to build a happy center, for children with Down syndrome, the angels that I know.

Further in this book, you will read a true story of **a toddler** with Down syndrome who inspired me. Remembering her on difficult days, when I was frustrated and not wanting to continue writing, she gave me the courage to continue. She lit my heart with a tiny spark. It was why I decided to continue writing this, no matter how frustrating or embarrassing it ends up.

By the way, I am an immigrant and a dreamer! When I started this book, early on I realized, the dream of writing a best-selling book and building a children's center, the dream of inspiring English-language audiences and helping others by that book is just too much for an *ESL student! Many times, I thought about giving up, but that spark didn't let me. It ignited and warmed my heart again and again.

I had a dream. I'm still a dreamer, and this book is dedicated to all dreamers!

*   ESL refers to English as a Second Language

CHAPTER 2

How The Story Began

I remember one day I got a call from a real estate company to go for an interview. I went there, and an hour later, I got hired to photograph a number of their very luxurious properties. I was so happy. The pay would be very good, too.

The interview took place by the beach, and when I left, I had a big, big smile on my face. For a few moments, I felt like I was flying in the clouds over that beautiful beach with the seagulls.

For two or three minutes, anyway.

Everything was fantastic — until I saw my car! My smile faded from my face and my jaw dropped as I fell from the sky to the sidewalk.

Shooot, I hadn't thought about how my car was not suitable for this job. I had a beautiful and safe Volvo v70, which had a lot of room for all my equipment, but the car was old and getting something around 17 miles per gallon.

In an instant, I remembered the guy who interviewed me said that this job involves lots of driving around. For example, sometimes I might have to drive from a property in Coronado Island to a property in Rancho Santa Fe on the same day. That's about fifty miles, and that was not possible with my car.

I sat thinking on that beach for a few minutes and then came to the conclusion that I cannot do this job with this car. As I drove home, I was still thinking of different solutions. I loved that car, but driving about fifty miles twice a day was too much for that old car. It wasn't even economically feasible.

When I got home, still thinking about the costs of gasoline and the probable costs of car repairs, I walked to my mailbox, opened it, and the very first letter on top was a promotional invitation to buy a car from the bank where I had an account.

Was it a sign?

* * *

Some people may not agree, but I believe in a guiding force that leads whoever believes in it and whoever wants it. Please don't get me wrong! If you say, "Everyday, people receive dozens of such promotional mails." I know! You're right!

If you say, there has never been a divine guidance in your life and you don't believe in it, I know you are still right! You don't believe it. It doesn't exist for you. We'll agree to disagree. And why do you want to argue with a peaceful dude who has a mustache that looks like yoga pants?

One day, a rider who was a little bit drunk gave me this sticker as she laughed loudly. Imagine my face

I remember I looked at that mail and said to myself, "Don't even think about it! Last month, you spent all your cash savings to buy that very expensive equipment, and now you don't have even a hundred bucks in your savings, so you can't even make the monthly payments for a new car. Hey, you don't even think about it" ... I looked at that mail again and said to myself, "Okay...I'm done with my day, the branch is two minutes away, they are still open, and I'm just curious! Let's go and just inquire. I promise I'm not going to buy anything. I promise!"

I went to the bank and half an hour later, I came out having bought a new car! Two days later they called me to come and sign some paperwork and pick up the car.

* * *

I got a beautiful Toyota Prius, and you cannot imagine how happy I was! As soon as I got the car, I put a post about it on one of my social media pages. Don't laugh at me. I was just amazed with all the new technology in that car, so like a kid who has gotten an amazing new toy I just wanted to show it off to everyone!

Immediately, an acquaintance, who is a little nosy and not one of my favorite people, texted me.

-Shahrad: *Did you buy a new car?* [My face resembled that of the comedian Oliver Hardy looking into the camera, annoyed]

-Me: *Can you guess?*

-Shahrad: *I mean ... Why did you buy a new car?* [Imagine Oliver Hardy again]

-Me: *What! Why?*

[I remember the first week when I arrived in the States, he wanted to see me somewhere and he came and told me that he had heard many interesting stories about my creativity and that he would like to work with me. At first, I accepted, but little by little I found out that it's really a bad idea to have any partnership with him.]

-Shahrad: *I mean I just wanted to say congratulations. Did you buy that car for doing something?*

-Me: *Yes, to drive it!*

-Shahrad: *Oh, come on, Vasna! I just want to see if I can help you... Look, this car is really perfect for working at Uber and Lyft. Let me send you a referral invitation, then you can start working as a rideshare driver.*

-Me: *Why do you want to do it? What is your benefit?*

-Shahrad: *You will get a good bonus if ...*

-Me: *Buddy, I said what is YOUR benefit.*

-Shahrad: *Nothing... You know... It's a very good side job and it's perfect to make some extra money ... I mean, imagine, on your way home, you will give a ride to somebody ... It's really fun! ... I really don't get anything because I'm sure you cannot give enough rides in the first month so probably, I don't get any bonuses, but ...*

-Me: *Shahrad I need to go to bed. GOOD NIGHT!!* [Oliver Hardy again.]

After that exchange with Shahrad, I didn't care or even think about what he had told me. I just left that topic there. Two days later, Jahan, another friend of mine, called me to ask if I would meet him at his frozen yogurt store and give him some ideas about how he could attract more customers. When I got there, he came out to show me where to park my car. He saw my new car.

Jahan: Wow, that's nice, is it brand new?

Me: Almost! Just a few thousand miles was on it when I bought it.

Jahan: Perfect!! This is the best way to buy a car, when you buy it with less than 30,000 miles on it.

[He came to the front of the car and pointed to the hood.]

Jahan: … Open it. [I did] 'Let's see … Hmmm … Man, this car is good even for 300,000 miles …'It's a great investment, and you can even make a hundred thousand dollars from it easily!

[I knew that guy to be a smart dude who is completely aware of what he's doing or what he's saying, so I gave him a confused look.]

Me: Hundred thousand? What do you mean? … Honestly, I'm even a little concerned about making the monthly payments.

[He smiled and pointed to the other car, which was parked on the corner spot.]

Jahan: Look at that car. Up to now, I've made $ 170,000 off that car. Guess where I got the money for this store and this new side business?

Me: Siiiiide?!!

* * *

When we got to his store, he explained to me that it's been a couple of years since he has been working as an Uber/Lyft driver. He said although he has a new ice cream business now, he would prefer to hire an employee to have enough time to be a rideshare driver!

I couldn't believe what he was saying, or maybe I didn't want to believe it because with many upcoming payments and bills, believing that could push me into a profession that I didn't feel good about. Something deep in my mind was telling me not to believe it. Something like a bad memory or a phobia.

Nobody was in the store except Jahan, me, and a very young employee. Jahan called over to that young girl, and for a few seconds she listened to Jahan's instructions. Then she clocked out and left.

[Jahan went to the back of the counter and turned to me.]

Jahan: Would you like a smoothie?

Me: No thank you; hmm…maybe water.

[He brought me a bottle of water and looked at my face and said]

Jahan: So? What do you think?

Me: Man, that's not something that I can do.

[Jahan looked shocked.]

Jahan: You cannot give me some advertising ideas?

Me: Oh, no no no, I mean yes! Sure, I can. Don't worry about it, there is a high school nearby, you just need to use a daily sales strategy with some discount coupons. I will help you to design flyers and coupons.

Jahan: So, you cannot do something else?

Me: Yeah, actually, I thought you were talking about doing rideshare business … I'm just not able to do that, and I don't want to ruin my car.

[Jahan went back to the counter again, brought a bowl of strawberries and replaced the empty strawberry bowl in front of the refrigerator and as he was working, he turned his head toward me and asked...]

Jahan: Why did you buy that car?

Me: These days, I am doing real estate photography, I need to drive a long distance between the properties and my previous car …

Jahan: Look, I'm working for both of those rideshare companies. In both of those apps, there is a feature that you can use to ask the system to give you riders in your direction...

Me: Buddy, I cannot do it. … Honestly … I don't believe that I can make money from this job. Simply, it's not a job for me. I don't know how to do it.

[Jahan looked at me in surprise. He pointed to a bottle of water.]

Jahan: This water cost me ten cents, and I sell it for one buck. Do you think that you can find a way to make $10 out of this bottle of water?

[I scratched my head a little]

Me: Hmmm, probably I can. I mean, I can try …

Jahan: Exactly! You can try!

[He moved closer to me and showed me his last year's tax form on his cellphone.]

Jahan: Basically, you can make around one dollar each mile/minute. Look! I made this much money last year, see my tax forms… it's real …

[He looked into my eyes.]

Jahan: Don't forget that whether you like the rideshare business or not, you will put a lot of miles on your car, maybe 100,000 miles. Imagine each week you drive five times from San Diego to L.A., so it's better to make $100k on your way.

Me: Hundred thousand dollars? Oh, come oooon! Are you kidding me?

Jahan: Buddy, I know you. If you can make $10 out of that bottle of water, I'm sure you also can make $100k easily.

Me: Whaaattt?

As I was leaving Jahan's store, he told me that he just sent me an invitation to start working for both Uber and Lyft. He also explained, in full, what bonuses we both would receive. We walked out toward my car, and he reminded me of the day we were getting to a place together. He told me that he believed I was a good driver, and he assured me that because I am a fast learner and a hard worker, I could easily earn $100,000 as a rideshare driver while I was using my car for my photography job. He thought I could do it before I drove my car 100,000 miles.

… I was thinking, "Huh that's too good to be true", but …

Jahan was right! I made it!

I earned that money, and, in this book, you will see how!

* * *

Jahan was kind of right when he said that I am a good driver, but only when I was driving alone! In fact, I had a phobia. A ridiculous fear about having somebody in my car while driving! The story of where this fear came from is also a funny story which I am about to share, but first I want to emphasize that I never ever could imagine one day I can make something out of driving. It was like a joke to me!

The story begins from the country I came from, Iran! A country where most men have a lot of confidence in driving, too much confidence!

Men in Iran have an interesting reason for that confidence. It is simply because they experience many incredible scenes every day, literally every day!

I mean you should see to believe it! I remember seeing funny footage that a few young tourists had recorded. They were screaming with excitement, "Oh no! Oh Noooo! Oh my God! Wow! Ohhhh! Stop, Stop, STOP! OMG, it is like PlayStation! … What video quality!"

Tehran is an amazing metropolis where people are not interested in pushing the brake!

Anyway, I remember the first month when I got my driver's license. I was driving very carefully, but little by little, the atmosphere of that fast city made me feel like I was a professional racer.

Four months after I got my driver's license, for the first time my father sat in the car with me as I drove. He is a lovely father, but as a passenger, he has terrible habits. First, he always wants to choose the route, and most of the time while he is giving directions, he gets super excited himself, so he talks loud and almost yells. I'm fine with his yelling, but the worst part is that sometimes he changes his mind about directions at the last possible moment.

I remember once, I was ready to go one way at the fork on the ramp and he suddenly changed his mind. I had to do a very dangerous maneuver to avoid missing the exit. One of those maneuvers which can ruin the rate of any rideshare driver! His reaction and when he told me that he would never give me his car again kept me from driving for several weeks.

Although my father had said, he would never give me his car again and never sit in a car when I'm driving, a few weeks later, he called me and said we need to go to the airport to pick up one of his friends who was coming from the U.S. Something happened on that day and that afterwards I didn't feel good when someone was in my car.

That guest was screaming in traffic, and I don't know why!

Since then, I feel like I'm a perfect driver when I'm alone, but not when somebody else is in my car! Anyway, I remember the next year I bought a brand-new car and the first week of having that car I had a first date with Lili, whom I had met on social media. We agreed to have dinner at a restaurant, but unfortunately it was a rainy evening. I picked up Lili, a light music was playing in my car and the rainy weather was almost nice, but for some reason that I didn't know, Lili wasn't feeling very well. For no more than two seconds, I looked at Lili from the corner of my eye and then...

BOOOOM! ... Believe it or not, as I looked to Lili the driver of the car in front of me decided to stop completely in the middle of the highway!

OMG! I slammed on the brakes, but it was too late, and I rear-ended the other car.

I still remember that frighteningly comical picture of Lili's nose pushed to the windshield, just like a funny sticker! Oh God, that accident may have shaped or added to my phobia!

Years later, when one of my screenwriting teachers suggested that I work as a taxi driver for a week to get to know the people and find an idea for a "road movie" screenplay, I made many excuses and finally turned down the offer.

There was only one simple reason ... I was scared to do that! Driving a taxi never even entered my mind. Those little but ridiculous incidents caused my phobia. The phobia of driving while someone else is in my car!

* * *

The day after my talk with Jahan, I went to take pictures of a property. I knew that "refer to drive" invitation link would expire soon, but I didn't want to think about it.

I was driving on a secluded road outside the city toward the location and various thoughts were running through my mind. Particularly those days I was working on a short movie screenplay. It was in English, a horror movie about the "Dark Web". I never liked making a horror movie, but I wanted to try filmmaking in the United States. So, I thought it was the only genre I could choose at the moment. I believed I could make a horror movie for cheap, maybe in an abandoned warehouse with a minimum of actors and actresses. Also, most importantly with minimal dialogue between the characters! Writing dialogue... another fear!

Honestly, writing dialogue in English was one of my biggest obstacles in making a movie. I had the necessary equipment. I know how to shoot. I could edit the scenes. I had my story, and I even knew a group of acting students who would join for the experience. But I couldn't write realistic dialogue between my characters. Whatever I wrote sounded fake, and the script didn't work well. I needed to learn people's everyday conversation.

* * *

I was still struggling with different thoughts. I wondered where I could hear real people talking without any filters, where I could learn ... where...

Suddenly, a memory flashed in my mind, a memory about my screenwriting teacher. I remember he told the class, "Hey guys, *you cannot make something look real if you don't know about it. You need to hear and sense it to get the idea for writing.*" I remember he gave an assignment about writing all the conversations that we may hear on public transportation, then he suggested I drive a taxi for my assignment!

As I said before, I believe in a guiding power, but most of the time I struggle with trusting my guts. Instead, I try to use my brain like a rational person. It is kind of funny. I believe in that power but sometimes, privately, I argue with that in my mind like a monologue. Especially when I need to find my way or when I want to make an important decision. I remember I refused to do the assignment which my professor designated for me. He asked me why. I gave too many excuses. I said, "*because as a passenger when we share a ride, other passengers don't make that much conversation. I cannot keep paying for taxi rides. I have my own car and my phobia won't let me work as a driver.*"

To which my professor replied. "*Okay, you need work as a taxi driver for a week. Son, you should learn how to start and lead a conversation. I won't force you, but having a phobia isn't an excuse. If you don't face your fear, that will always be in your way. If you want big achievements, face your fear.*"

I told him: *Professor, I will try that, but not now! Please change my assignment. You can even give me an extra assignment*!

* * *

Back on that narrow road outside of the city, the thoughts were loud in my mind. It was like a party. I started a monologue:

"*Okay, let's review what I have here. I'm going to take shots of that property no matter how far it is. This is my job. I get good money for it. Forget about what Shahrad and Jahan told me...I will be able to pay my car's payments easily. This job does not put that much mileage on my car, and I don't like to drive when somebody is in my car... I don't think rideshare driving helps me learn to write dialogues! Even if it helps, I don't want it! Okay? God, please stop flashing the memory of that professor's assignment in my mind! I'm not able to be a rideshare driver! And most importantly, I don't want anyone to sit in my beautiful car at all! They may ruin my car, I will not leave my shore of peace, and I will not ruin my beautiful car. So, dear, I'm sorry but you cannot force me. Period!"*

Craaaacks!!

A rock from somewhere came and cracked my windshield. I couldn't believe it, there was no car even on that road, so where did that stone come from?

I pulled the car to the side and stared at the crack, then looked at the sky and frowned for a few seconds.

The next day, I was driving on the highway to the address of a large villa north of San Diego. I would occasionally look at the cracked glass while driving. I really couldn't believe it happened to my new car less than a week after buying it. I especially couldn't believe the timing. It got cracked exactly right after that inner monologue. While I was driving, Jahan called. He wanted to see if I had worked on the advertising plans for his store, and he wanted to remind me that the invitation link would expire soon. We had a short conversation, and I told him I would call him back later.

Just when I hung up, I started another inner monologue: *"I'm sorry, dear Jahan, I'd like to help you with your store, but I won't call you back because you want to keep reminding me of that expiring link and keep bugging me to start working as a rideshare driver. I'm sorry, dude, nobody can force me. Perio..."*

CRAaaaaaaaaCKSS!!

I know this is really unbelievable, but another rock hit my car's windshield and cracked it again! I was so shocked that I didn't think to look where the rock came from, and which car was guilty.

Before that day, I had been driving for almost thirteen years. It had never occurred to me that a rock from nowhere could break my car's windshield. All of a sudden, two days in a row, my car's windshield got cracked. My new, darling car. OMG!

The next day, I was so upset that I called in sick for my job and canceled the photo session. For many hours, I stayed in bed, upset, and angry. Somehow, I was angry with myself. In the evening, I wanted at least to do something, so I decided to go out and do a little grocery shopping.

On the way to the store, I thought to myself: *"This was just an accident which happened because of* **Murphy's Law.** *I should stop these crazy monologues, stop thinking about "rideshare jobs" and the cracks on my windshield. I said to myself: "Tomorrow I will go and change the windshield, and nothing will happen after that. Nobody can force me to do anything when I don't like it.*

I parked the car, locked the door, and then repeated to myself, *"Nobody can force me, period!*

The grocery store was in a shopping center that also had a barbershop, a bar, a dental office, and a liquor store. It was around 8 p.m. and was getting darker and darker. I shopped in the store for about an hour and little by little my mood improved, like school children who had fun on a rainy day. I was enjoying the thunder sound of the automatic water spray system on the vegetables. That idea is so interesting to me, that every spray made me happier.

* *Murphy's Law refers to very negative thinking. More details in Chapter 17.*

When I left the store, I was in a positive mood, and I kept repeating to myself, *"Nobody, period. Nobody, yes, nobody Perrr..."*

I had arrived at my car. The photos below show what I saw!

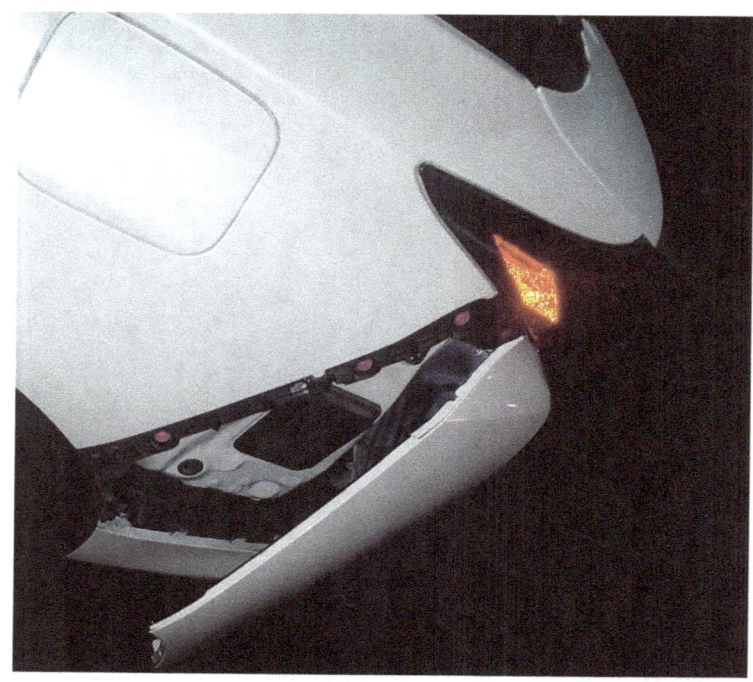

It looked like a drunk driver who had probably come out of the bar, backed into my car.

I decided, I had better apply for the rideshare job before the guiding power destroys my darling car completely. Period!

CHAPTER 3

My First Day!

After fixing my car, I applied to drive for Uber and Lyft, by using the new links that Jahan sent me. I passed the background checks both companies required and all the other necessary steps, so I became officially ready to work as a rideshare driver.

Although I usually like to start new adventures and I had all the required items, I was not mentally ready for it. For the first few days, I didn't want to turn on the app to try it. I made up excuses in my mind, saying to myself something like: *"Okay, okay but not today, maybe tomorrow!"*

One day, I had a photo shoot at a Coronado Island villa, but at the last minute, the owner canceled the session. I had nothing to do for the rest of the day, so I drove toward my home, but when I saw an exit to Downtown/Airport, I took it because I remembered a friend of mine was working very close to that area, preparing a stage for a big concert that weekend. I decided to go and meet my friend and maybe I could give him a little help setting up his equipment. The stage was on Harbor Drive, close to the airport. I went to a gas station to fill my tank and call my friend to see if he could get me into his working area.

It was a hot summer day, and I was thirsty. I went into the store, and I got an ice-cold bottle of water. The gas station employee said that "it's two water bottles for three dollars", so I told her, "Okay, charge me for two. I will give one of those to my friend. He will love it."

I walked out of the store, got into my car, put the bottles on the cup holders, and called my friend, but he didn't answer. I left him a voicemail: *"Hey man, I'm close to your workplace and I'd love to come and see your stage. I'll stay around here for a few more minutes. If you get this message in the next 15 minutes, call me back."*

That week was an extremely busy one in San Diego, with a lot of events going on, so the airport was busy as well. While I was at that gas station, bored and pissed off that he didn't return my call, I tried to entertain myself with my phone. I tapped the new rideshare app and started playing with it. I touched the "Go" bottom of that app and …

Driiiiiing!!!

Driiiiiiiiiiiiiiiing!!!

A ride request popped up on my screen. The sound was so loud and shocking that, like a terrified child, I unconsciously tapped it to prevent a disaster! As a result, I accepted my first ride!

I felt like a kid who was afraid to swim and now got thrown into the pool. The ride request was from the airport, but I was not even inside the airport queue, in that waiting lot where all the drivers should stay to get a ride request.

I spent almost 2 minutes trying to cancel the trip, but I couldn't figure out how. Then I thought if I ignored the trip for a minute, hopefully the passenger would cancel it, but since it was a very busy day at the airport, he didn't cancel it.

I got out of the gas station. I had to go to the airport because the rider, Mike, was waiting for me!

* * *

Airports are usually a most complicated place for novice drivers. At San Diego International Airport, the rideshare passenger loading zone is right under a ramp where the navigation commands become even more confusing.

I remember two times in a row I went the wrong way. Finally, he called me.

Mike: Hey, I'm Mike where are you man?

Me: Oh hi… sorry there was something wrong with the app, but I got it! No worries, I'm coming right now, and I will be there in a few minutes.

Mike: Okay good, I have a white shirt and black pants on, no luggage, and I will shake my hand when I see you okay? You just drive slowly.

Me: Perfect, see you soon.

That day was a hot day, the AC was on, and the inside of the car was like heaven. As soon as I turned to the zone, I saw a guy with white shirt and black pants, no luggage, was shaking his hand and coming toward me. I stopped and he jumped in and said:

Passenger: Oooh man, finally. Wow, what a cold clean car…

Me: Sorry Mike, for that little delay, but I'm going to drive fast, and you will be in your place very soon.

Passenger: …wow you even have cold water here! No problem, dude.

Me: Yes, please help yourself.

He gladly took one of those very cold waters that I had bought from the gas station. I quickly got to the second lane and drove fast to the exit, and in a few minutes, we were more than a mile away from the airport. We got onto Interstate 5, and that was when my phone rang. It was Mike!

Mike: Hey man where arrrre you?

Me: Excuse me? Who is this??

*Mike: Oooh GOD, I'm Mike and it is F***** 20 minutes I'm waiting for you.*

[I looked to the guy in the car and asked him:]

Me: Are you Mike?

Jorge: I'm Jorge and you must be Amit Sikh, Toyota Prius white, correct?

Mike: OhhhH, God dammit.

Me: Mike I'm so sorry…listen … this guy … we are in highway… what can I do …

*Mike: … [He was shouting loudly on the phone] … If I see you, I'll f*** you up!*

Me: Oh, Dear no! … Hold on, Don't … it hard! … Can you please … cancel… Mike…

[Mike angrily was shouting at me something like "If I see you, I'll f*** you up!" It shocked me so much that I couldn't think of a proper English sentence in my mind, Jorge could hear Mike, too, I wanted to respond something like "Dear Sir, please don't make this problem more difficult, but I was shocked and forgot all the English I knew, I said, "Oh dear, is it so hard?" which made Jorge think I was making fun of Mike, and he exploded in laughter. Mike let out a huge roar of anger, hung up the phone and in a few seconds, he cancelled the trip, I looked to Jorge and asked him:]

Me: Oh maaaan, why did you say you are Mike!?

Jorge: Did I?

Me: Oh God, why did you laugh!? Oh, my Gooood, I have to pull over somewhere and you need to leave.

Jorge: Man, do you want to drop me off here in the middle of the highway? C'mon, my place is just two exits away from here. I'll give you the directions.

[When we got to his address, he gave me a $20 bill.]

Jorge: Thank you and sorry.

Me: What's this? I should not accept cash fare.

Jorge: This is not the fare, it is a tip.

Me: They told us that we should say to the riders that tipping is not necessar...

[He took another $20 bill out of his wallet.]

Jorge: Oh, I forgot... Thank you for that cold water of heaven.

While I looked at him confused, he put the bills on the front seat, blinked at me, and then he left! I was shocked and confused and still staring at those two twenty-dollar bills and suddenly

Driiiiiiiiiing!!!

Driiiiiiiiiiiiiiing!!!

Guess what I did?? I panicked and tapped the screen again, so my second trip got accepted!

I looked thoughtfully at those $20 bills on the front seat, then I turned my head to the app. I was completely confused because this new "pick-up" point was the same as my current location! I was scratching my head then all of sudden an old man opened the car door and got to the back seat!

The old man frowned and looked at my confused face:

Old man: Are you Vasna?

Me: Yes.

Old man: I'm Mike.

*Me: Oh F***!*

My second passenger's name was Mike as well. I was terrified that this was the Mike coming to take revenge and do what he said! When he saw me looking at him in confusion, he asked if I was a new driver, then without waiting for my answer, he told me to follow the navigation, but when we get close to his destination, he would show me a faster and better route!

When he said he would give me the address, it reminded me of the way my father gave me directions. I was subconsciously terrified, so because of that stress, I was shaking, and I took the wrong exits four times in a row. Then I touched my phone screen and mistakenly ended the trip. After ending the trip, because I no longer had the address, I had to pull over. I pulled into the first safe place at the corner of a street. When I stopped, I turned to him with a tear in the corner of my eye.

Me: I ended the trip by mistake.

Mike: No worries! I need to go to my dentist on Clairemont Mesa Boulevard, but I can get another...

Me: Oh really? The dental office next to the barbershop?

Mike: Yes.

Me: Oh good, it's close to my home. I know exactly where it is.

Mike: Actually, it's a little late. I prefer ...

Me: Please ... No worries. We'll get there before your appointment. Would you like cold water? I have ice cold water here.

[I offered the second bottle of water to Mike. There was still a piece of ice floating inside the bottle. I guess he felt pity for me and of course it was late to request a new ride. He seemed thirsty, so he smiled, took the water, and said:]

Mike: You don't get paid for the remaining distance.

Me: That's okay, if you let me, I'd like to give you a free ride as a friend.

Mike: Do you want me to help you find the direction?

Me: NO PLEASE! Not at all!

Mike: All right, I need to be there before 2 p.m. [It was about 1:40 p.m.]

Me: Let's go!

[I took a deep breath and whispered to myself, "No one is in the car, just do your usual driving toward home."]

When we got there, it was ten minutes before 2. He seemed very pleased with that cold water and the timely arrival. Before getting out of the car, he took out a $20 bill from his wallet and said: "You are a good and fast driver! It's just a little gift as a friend," I stared at him, shocked and confused, but before I could say anything he put the money on the front seat next to the other two banknotes and ran to the dentist office.

When he got out of the car, the very first thing I did was to double-check to make sure the app was off and wasn't going to pop up again. Then I said to myself, "That's enough, that is really enooooough! It's not your job. You don't have to be in that stressful situation again. That's not your job, man, and it was your last crazy adventure. Perioooo..."

Beeeeeeeepp !!

Beeeeeeeeeeeeeepp !!!

The horrible honking sound coming from a huge pickup truck didn't even allow me to say the word *"period"* completely. Apparently, the spot where I stopped, to let Mike leave, was right in front of one of the driveways. A truck driver wanted to express his anger at my mistake with the sound of that awful honk.

I moved my car a little forward, and the driver of the truck turned to the street. He showed his middle finger to me and drove away. What a day! Right after that, I made sure that I parked the car in the right spot. I turned off the engine, got out of the car and with great intensity and anger started screaming and shouting, just like a crazy man!

While shouting, I suddenly realized this is exactly where I parked the car a few days ago in front of that bar where that drunk driver damaged my car. I looked and I realized a little farther away was a parked police car, and then I realized the police officer had just come out of the store and was walking toward me. It seemed he was going to ask me why I was yelling. I know it sounds very silly, but at that moment, I looked to the sky and said: *"Okay, okay, let's have a deal: Don't make any more problems for me and I will keep on working this stressful job. Okay?"*

After asking me a few questions, the police officer left. I sat down on the hot asphalt for a few minutes, next to the car, which calmed me down. I looked like a child who finally gave up and accepted the fact that he had to do his damn homework. When I felt a little better, I went into the store and picked up whatever cold-water bottles were in the fridge and bought them all!

That day, I made several other trips. I remember because I was kind of nervous and I wanted to increase the passengers' tolerance for possible mistakes that I'll do while driving, as soon as they got into my car, I offered them a cold bottle of water and a nice smile! The riders' reactions were very interesting. Almost all of them said something like *"Wow, a super clean car and super cold water!"* Almost all of them also asked me, *"How long have you done this job?"* Maybe they thought how professional I was. I remember I told the first person who asked that question: *"This is my first day of working!"* When I said that, I immediately saw that she got a little scared and nervous, so as a result the whole time, I was very nervous as well, and it caused me to make a series of mistakes.

After that experience, I joked with everyone who asked the same question, telling them that I am one of the top ten drivers in the U.S. They smiled, but the effect of the sentence, even as a joke, was amazing. Most of them enjoyed their trip in silence, so I could imagine that nobody was in my car, and it was helping me to drive more confidently.

That day I made almost $100 in fares and $110 in cash tips. For half a day, it was not bad at all.

* * *

When I came to the U.S., I was such a bad driver that even my cousin didn't like to sit in my car. In a little over a year, I had over 5,000 five-star trips, and many riders said that they really would like to be in my car again and again. Now, according to the companies' statistics, I am one of the best drivers in the United States! [I mean according to the information provided to me by a few driver support agents at the hub.]

After the first day, I was convinced that I could do this rideshare job on my way to my photography job to make a little more money and maybe get ideas or learn something useful for my screenplay. That was the initial goal.

* * *

The next day, I went to the real estate company office because I needed to talk to the manager and hand in a few extensive files. Plus, I needed to talk about coordinating my schedules in order to shoot at the best time of day for lighting. The manager told me that one of the appointments was cancelled again, and I didn't have another photo shoot until next week, so my weekend got started sooner.

On the way back home, I needed to do some grocery shopping to fill up my fridge because I had a potluck party with friends that weekend. I don't know why, but something in my mind made me go to a different shopping center.

I had a pack of mineral water on my list, but at the store I saw a four-pack for $9.99, which was a good deal. I thought to myself, *"Okay, I'm going to need that because we have a potluck at the beach and the weather is hot, so let's buy that, it's a good deal."*

I usually put a few bottles of water in the freezer the day before I go to the beach, then take them out of the freezer shortly before they completely freeze. The ice in the bottle slowly melts at the beach, so I have very cold water all day long. When I got home, out of habit, I put one of the water packs in the freezer.

That evening at home, I was working on my screenplay. I needed to find a unique and strong starting point for a family quarrel. I was thinking to myself that I need to see the starting point of a real family drama, one where a small spark leads a calm person to explode in a few seconds. One of the characters in my screenplay should get to that explosion point, and the last incident should be very rudimentary and ridiculous but real enough to lead her to that point of anger where she goes to the dark web to hire a mercenary to get revenge.

I didn't like to copy something from a movie or TV show. The drama's starting point that I created in my mind did not make sense to an American friend who I had asked for feedback.

I was tired, so I stopped working and laid down. A funny memory of my grandmother came to my mind. When I was a child, my grandmother on my mother's side used to say that husbands are the cause of all family quarrels. My father was kidding with her and said: *" ... but I am a good husband for your daughter."* My grandmother answered, *"The place of good husbands like you is in the pot!"* And my father asked mischievously, *"Oh, dear, so what about a bad husband?"* And my grandmother laughed and said, *"Of course, under the pot!"*

* * *

I woke up to the ringing sound of my phone. A friend of mine let me know that the beach plan had been canceled because they needed to go to Orange County for a surprise party. I had bought a lot of food and I had already put one of the water packs in the freezer.

I was so upset, not because I wasn't invited to the surprise party but because it felt like anyone could cancel something in my life. Recently, I had not been free enough to have some exciting and fun adventures, and many people had control over my life. That was not my favorite way to live. Anyway, I frowned and went to take the water bottles out of the freezer, and then I left them in the sink to melt. I was pissed off. I went back to my bed, and I was thinking about my script, which also was not going well at all.

After half an hour, Jahan called me. I had completely forgotten to design his ads and coupons. I apologized to him.

Me: Sorry, man, I really don't know why I haven't done anything in the last two days ...

Jahan: Are you kidding me? You did a great job yesterday.

Me: What do you mean?

Jahan: We both received a three-buck bonus for each ride that you gave on Lyft. Good job! ... Did you work on Uber as well?

Me: Yes, I did.

Jahan: Perfect! Uber will give all the bonuses after completing the Quest trips. Keep doing your great work … 'Don't spend your time designing the coupon at all, too many events are held this weekend. I'm downtown right now. A festival is being held here, a lot of money and a lot of fun entertainment. Come here right now!

After his call I put all my water bottles in a cooler and said to myself: *"Fun? Okay, let's go!"*

* * *

That weekend, I had a unique and unforgettable time. I made around a thousand dollars in fares and tips, and you won't believe how many funny and weird stories happened in my car. Most were interesting and enjoyable, but some were very challenging and scary.

I don't really know if I was lucky or not, but that week I had three family dramas in a row, which of course helped me a lot with my screenplay, but drama in a car is the last thing that a rideshare driver likes.

God bless my grandmother! The first story happened because of a husband!

The story began when I was downtown, I received a ride share request via UberPool, which gives passengers the option to share a ride for a more affordable price. I accepted and went to pick up a man, around age of 45-50, who was a little angry.

He sat in the back seat. I immediately offered him a bottle of ice water when I saw his face. He looked at the water and said, *"Wow, there's a piece of ice floating in it."*

He took the bottle, and I was happy that I did something to please him. Then the app added another rider. I drove to the front of a fancy restaurant to pick up that second passenger. That restaurant was a perfect place to go on a date, and the second passenger was a lady. She stood in front of that place looking toward us and saw that somebody was already in the back seat. Since it was dark, she couldn't see the face of the other passenger, so she got in the front seat.

I had already offered a bottle of water to a rear passenger and as my usual way, after making sure that I picked the right passenger, I offered her the second bottle of cold water which I had in my cup holder.

[I learned something very important here, which later I will share with you on the tip pages.]

She looked thirsty, and at first, wanted to accept the water, but she paused for a moment, and with a kind smile she asked with surprise,

-*"What is this?"*

The man in the back seat answered:

Back Seat Man: She doesn't like such cold water from you!

Me: Excuse me!?

Front Lady: Oh no, oh God … What the hell are you doing here? Are you following me?

[Then she looked at me.]

Front lady: Are you with him?

Me: Excuzzz …

Backseat Man: Am I following you? It is only a week since I got rid of you, and I feel free! Why should I follow you? Hah!

Front lady: I was happy thinking I won't see your face again! … You can ruin anything … I'm glad I divorced you.

Backseat man: I ruin anything? You ruin everything, including this stupid's water?

Me: Ex…ki…use…me!?

*Front lady: Water…? You are together? Oh yes, hah, I see… You arrrre together … What is in this water? … Pull over this F****** CAR …*

[She tried to open the door.]

Me: Excu No…noo !! … Don't … kiuz … oh wait … oooz … ooozme … Oh God!!

She doesn't like cold water!

Do you think I'm a lucky screenwriter who could experience a weird family drama this close? Imagine having a recently divorced couple sharing a ride!

* * *

The second family drama that I witnessed up close, happened the next night after the first one. I remember when I got to the pickup point, two women and two men were waiting for me. As soon as I stopped, one of the women lunged to the front. The second woman, who also wanted the front seat, angrily sat in the back seat right behind me. That woman was followed by a panicked man, a poor guy who got placed somehow between two women in the middle of the backseat and after him, the second man got into the car. This guy, I later found out was the boyfriend of the woman in front.

In order to make sure that I had the right passengers in my car, I asked them:

Me: Excuse me, what is the account name?

Middle man: Dave, I'm Dave.

Front Woman: Yeah. He is my brother, and this is my ride!

Backseat Woman: Haha, he is my husband!

I started the trip. The car's atmosphere was clearly tense. Dave tried to change the atmosphere by telling a stupid joke, but it didn't work. When we stopped behind the first traffic light, I just wanted to help that poor man, so I told them:

Me: Hey, guys, I have very cold bottles of water, if anyone wants to cool dow...

Front Woman: Yes, this is my water... You should talk to me, I'm your boss and everybody's b ...

Back seat Woman: That's my water, don't touch it!

Me: I have two of those bott...

Each lady jumped and grabbed a bottle of water! Right at that moment, the second man opened the car door and fled. The cars behind me started to honk. I was shocked and didn't know what's really going on. The back seat lady said: *"Join your F***** boyfriend!"* That sentence was enough to change the family drama into a war, a cold and wet war! The women started splashing water on each other. The only thing that came to my mind was to stop the car in a safe place. The right side of my body was completely wet.

With a strong but respectful tone, I told the woman in the front seat that if she didn't calm down, she would have to leave the car. She showed one of her fingers to me and left the car. I won't say which finger I saw again in front of my eyes. I only say that unfortunately it wasn't the thumbs-up sign!

After she left, I looked at Dave's face, then I set off for the destination. Water droplets were all over the car's interior. Poor Dave wanted to say something.

Dave: Man, you did a good job!

Dave's wife: You should ...

Me: No problem.

Dave: What's your job, man?

Dave's wife: Uh, can't you guess what his job is? Your sister just ruined his car!

Me: I am a photographer. This is kind of my side job these days. I write a screenplay as well.

Dave: Ooh, cool, a photographer.

Dave's wife: Yeah, he is going to take photos of all the mess which your sister made and send it to the company. You will get charged for it and that makes me happy!

[When she said that, Dave started to dry the doors and windows.]

Me: Don't worry, man. Do not stain the window. Let it dry.

Dave: Ok, I just wanted to do something for ... You know, I have a company and we are working on copyright processes... if you need help...

Me: Do you mean copyright for book or screenplay or photos?

Dave: Almost everything. Do you write stories?

Me: Hmmm, screenplay.

Dave's wife: As soon as we arrive, he will take photos of your sister's mess and you will pay for it!

As soon as they got out of the car, I started to take photos. Dave saw it and gave me a confused and sad look. I told him:

Me: Don't worry, I don't report you to the company, I'm a photographer and I like to take photos of everything. I don't know, but maybe one day I'll use my photos somewhere! Just don't worry. I will come to you maybe for copyright of a photo novel or something else!

He showed one of his fingers to me and left. This time, I'll tell you which one it was: a thumb!

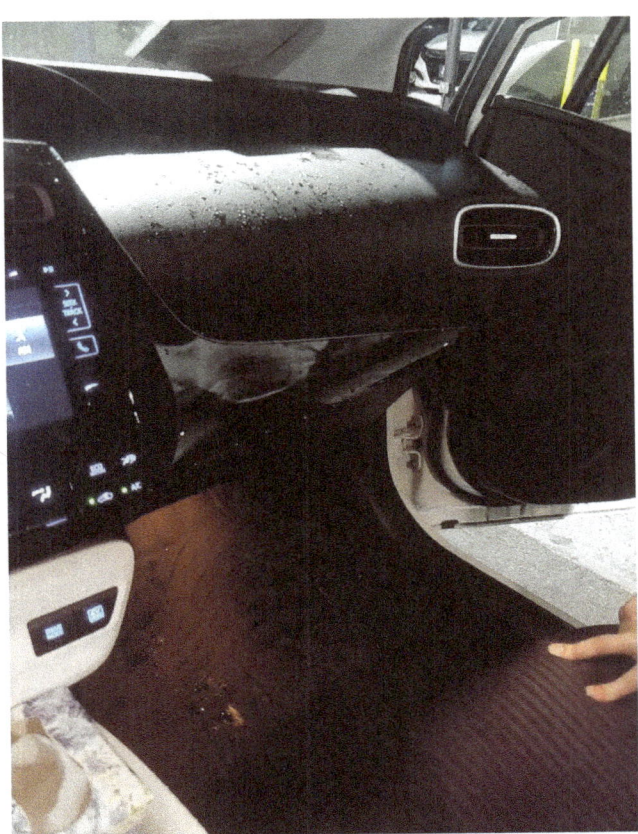

Dave is the guy who helped me with this book's copyright process!

* * *

I know this is crazy and unbelievable, but the third drama took place the same night and right after dropping off Dave. I was wiping off and drying the water from my car's interior. I was thinking that's enough drama for tonight when another ride request popped up. I said to myself, *"Okay, let's have a happy final trip and a happy ending for tonight!"* I went to the pickup point, and four sexily dressed ladies got into my car. Soon after the trip started, the lady in the front seat spoke up.

Front Lady: What a stylish car you have, but why is it wet all around? First, I thought somebody threw up in your car, but when I saw even the sunroof was wet, I know it's not because of throwing up.

Me: You are smart … also sharp-eyed!

[One of the ladies in back seat spoke up angrily.]

Back Lady: Yes, and she wants to talk with all the men.

Front lady: Don't listen to her. You didn't say why it's wet everywhere.

Me: Two ladies were fighting in my car with water!

Front Lady: Oh really? Are you kidding me?

Me: No kidding!

Front Lady: By the way, I'm Marie.

*Back Lady: You are not Marie. I am Marie. You are Maria b****!*

Me: Oh, okay, nice to meet you both.

*Front Lady: Don't listen to this little b**** … Why were they fighting with each other?*

Me: I guess over a man. The man who was sitting in the middle!

Back Lady: Hah, maybe we should do it, too.

Front Lady: Shut up, you bastard! That man asked for my number, not yours. He looked at me and said Marie's number, but you bastards scared him away.

[At that moment, the third woman angrily said:] *"You scared off the whole group of them"*, and the fourth woman started screaming. They started fighting, a terrible beating that I have never seen before!

If you think it is not possible for such a serious beating to happen, or if you think all the quarrels are over men, you are wrong in both cases. Look at the next picture.

I guess this fight was over a woman! Please don't blame me, I am a driver but also a photographer!
As a photographer I love to capture these special moments!

Tip Pages

The amenities you provide for your passengers have a significant effect on your rating and on the tip you receive, but be careful how and when you offer the amenities.

Regardless of your good intentions, sometimes offering a bottle of water at the wrong time may cause discomfort and inconvenience.

In this book, I will talk about the items that will have a huge impact on your rating and tip. And most importantly, I will share whatever I learned about the best time and best way to provide each item to achieve your desired result: a higher rating and a bigger tip!

To begin with, two of the most important items are water bottles and cell phone chargers.

For the water bottles, you can have a small cooler in your trunk to keep all the bottles and bring only two for each ride. Place them in a very clean and sterile place, such as in the cup holders near you, where the passenger can see them. I usually keep the bottles in two paper cups just to keep them cool and not let the moisture soak in my car's cup holder. The paper cups are only to temporarily store the bottles and are not to be given to passengers.

Keep the phone chargers connected and ready to use in front of the passenger seat.

The easiest and most effective way to present these two items to the passenger is at the beginning of the ride with a tone that seems like it is a routine and ordinary greeting. Just point out the places where the items can be found and let the passengers know that you have these items in the car and that they are very welcome to help themselves if needed.

Important note: **Never insist** or offer anything twice!

CHAPTER 4

The Birth Of A "Rideshare Writer"

The next week, I only had one scheduled day of work and only one photo shooting session. I don't remember why my schedule was like that. Maybe it was because of a holiday or something else, but I remember a group of friends were going on a cruise ship and I couldn't join them again.

I was feeling lonely. My sleep cycle had gotten very chaotic, and I had sleeping problems at night. This also was the time when my friend Mehrdad was preparing to immigrate to Germany. He was under a lot of stress, and I was one of his close friends who had immigration experience, so every day we were online chatting for almost two hours. We were almost 12 time zones apart, and those off time chats made my sleep problem even worse.

That week, many events, including a big festival, were taking place in San Diego. For a few days, I slept in the morning and chatted with my friend in the afternoon. Then having nothing interesting to do, I would work as a rideshare driver from something like 8 p.m. to 4 a.m.

That was an amazing, super-fun experience, especially for a night person who loves the moon, enjoys driving at night and enjoys fun adventures. The very good thing was that when I didn't have any passengers in my car, I would stop and take some photos of people's nightlife and those weird incidents that occurred around me.

I witnessed five strange incidents that happened right in front of my eyes, and almost all of those at 3 a.m. Thank God nobody got injured and I was able to take pictures of some of those scenes.

Every afternoon during the chat with my friend, I had at least two or three photos and funny stories to share with him. I was giving him stress relief for a few minutes. The first story started like this:

Me: Oh, man, ask what happened to me last night exactly at 3 a.m.

Mehrdad: What happened?

Me: I was driving next to a beautiful girl's car. She rolled down the window, so I thought maybe she wanted to say or ask something…

Me: She had a big smile on her face, and she was blinking and waving at me.

Mehrdad: Oooooh. Maybe she knew you from somewhere.

Me: Actually, at first, I thought the same, so I was driving next to her for 10-15 seconds and I waved back at her...

Mehrdad: So, what happened next?

Me: … But I didn't know her, and her smile was not looking normal … her clothes were not decent enough to cover her body… then …

Mehrdad: Hmmmmm … then?

Me: … Then I saw a police car turn into the street right behind us, so I immediately dropped my speed…

Mehrdad: Did the police pull her over?

Me: She did it by herself.

Mehrdad: What do you mean?

Me: When she passed my car while she was still smiling and waving her hand to a ghost … she drove to the sidewalk, hit a big tree, and popped her car's airbag.

Mehrdad: Really?

Me: The police car immediately turned on its lights and stopped the traffic. I pulled over to see if I could help, but … funny… she was okay and

Mehrdad: …and you looked at your watch, it was exactly 3 a.m.? Hahaha…Oh, come on, don't make up a story!

Me: No, seriously … the reason that I found out about the time was when the police officer mentioned it to his colleague.

Mehrdad: What did he say?

Me: He said, "Oh, another 3 a.m. accident!"

* * *

The very next day …

Me: Ask me what happened at 3 a.m.

Mehrdad: Another accident?

Me: Hahaha…a super ridiculous one.

Mehrdad: How?

Me: Can you believe it? A police car was blocking off the street and stopping the traffic. Suddenly, a man drove up and hit the police car's front door, right where it says: "To protect and serve."

Mehrdad: Oh shooooot, did you take a photo?

Me: Are you kidding me? The police officer was shocked and angry at the driver who was telling him something like, "Hey, man, you shouldn't park in the middle of the way!" I couldn't believe my eyes…I looked at the dash clock. It says 3 a.m.!

Really dude?! You hit my car?

* * *

Two days later, I text Mehrdad…

Me: guess what happened last night at 3a.m.?

Mehrdad: Stop joking please … it's not possible!

Me: Come on, check this out: A guy hit the fire hydrant. I took a photo just to show it to you. Look at this photo then check the details and see what time it was! [I sent the photo to him]

Explanation: This was another photo taken later from the same kind of accident! It was January, around three o'clock in the morning!

Mehrdad: Oooh! My God, no way dude! Man, that's crazy … Now it's a real mystery. We need to find out why all those accidents happened at 3 a.m.

Me: I found it!

* * *

That night, when I pulled over to take pictures of the water fountain, there was a fire truck and a police car. I looked at the policeman's face. He looked very nice and kind, so I thought I'd ask him about that mystery.

Me: Hello, sir, is everybody in that car, okay?

Officer: Hi, yes, they are.

Me: Wow, this is the first time that I see something like this. Did it just happen?

Officer: A few minutes ago.

Me: OMG! Do you mean it was around 3 a.m.? I cannot believe it! Sir, a quick question, please.

Officer: Go ahead.

Me: This week, I saw a few accidents around 3 a.m., and in one of them I heard a police officer say: "Oh, another 3 a.m. accident!" What does that mean?

Officer: Maybe it means…this week is a holiday, some people are at the bars until 2:30 a.m., which is the time that bars get closed, and around 2:15 a.m. people are being asked to finish their drinks and leave the bar. It's a common mistake people make. Some of them want to drive so they just buy one shot and spend their time chatting with friends without finishing their drink. Then, when it's time they drink their one shot quickly and they believe that they can get home before the shot can get into their system, but that shot can affect them faster than normal. The loss of control is not gradual. It is sudden, so usually these drivers hit something on the side of the road. They all get DUIs.

You just take one shot, and you get DUI, while others drank the whole night and get home, safe in a Lyft or Uber!

* * *

Mehrdad was not okay that day. He was struggling with an awful stress. He was heartbroken, and I knew why his heart was hurting so bad. I had experienced that feeling before. Migration is one of the most stressful things that can happen in life. To me, it feels like dying. Even if you go to heaven, you will still have to experience that painful death.

Most of the immigrants are forced to leave their country and they had to leave very dear things behind. A dear thing could even be a grave! A dear thing behind will make a gap in your heart forever!

No matter how successful you are, when you go to another country as an immigrant, most of the time you need to start from scratch! Start from nothing and with a gap in your heart!

The worst feeling is that sometimes you feel like you wasted your life up to that moment and you did nothing. You keep asking yourself, what can I accomplish in my life that is of value? Something that can give a meaning to my life, to my wasted life! Mehrdad was feeling like that, and I did too! For a while I was feeling like that.

* * *

Mehrdad had a niece, beautiful angel, a newborn with Down syndrome. A baby girl that Mehrdad and I both thought had a special spirit. Sometimes, Mehrdad sends her pictures and videos to me.

What made the kid so special to us was not her syndrome, but her daily strange interest and faithful commitment to counting the plastic flowers of a vase. A weird daily action of a baby!

As a joke with Mehrdad, instead of her name, I would call her *Golshomar* which in my first language means "flower counter." For this angel, it looks as if counting those flowers calmed her down. Or perhaps a responsibility. Or even a life goal. She counted those flowers every day even when she struggled with fever and her poor physical condition. I felt like she was a little princess, who was responsible for her flowers with all her heart. I thought to myself, "*the world could be a better place to live in if each of us did one small task with such responsibility and with all our hearts.*"

Sadly, Golshomar passed away at the age of 7 months while she counted her flowers for the last time.

Mehrdad didn't know what to do with his life and he had to leave Golshomar's grave behind.

* * *

When I told Mehrdad what the police officer said about the "3 a.m. mystery," we had already been chatting for almost two hours, and Mehrdad still eagerly was following the story. I remember before I started telling the stories, he was awfully stressed, heartbroken, and gloomy.

I felt happy and fulfilled because my stories made him forget about the hardships of his world for at least a few minutes, so I continued telling the stories.

Me: Man, guess what happened again?

Mehrdad: Accident!? You already told that story!

Me: Not that one. Unfortunately, another one happened to me!

Mehrdad: Nooooo waaaaay! Come on! You're kidding me, your new car?

Me: You know we have a new transportation system here, a few companies rent out scooters! You can use your cellphone...

Mehrdad: Yeah, I saw them already on Facebook. That idea looks very cool.

Me: Uhh, I had a passenger in my car, we were downtown, and he was in a rush. On a busy street, a young man and woman were riding a scooter next to us…

Mehrdad: Hahaha, probably they were faster than you guys...

Me: Ugh… Believe it or not, those lovers were feeling like they were on the Titanic!

Mehrdad: What do you mean?

Me: The Titanic movie! …They were acting like they were Rose and Jack, arms wide, flying on a scooter!

Mehrdad: O'oh!

Me: Suddenly, they lost their balance and hit the back door of my darling car, then they left the scooter and ran.

Mehrdad: Hahahahaha! LOL!

*Me: #$@& * ***

Mehrdad: What did you do?

Me: This was the first time that I was in such a situation. My passenger was in a hurry. I had no experience, but I will definitely research on what to do in an accident like that.

Mehrdad: So, what are you going to do?

Me: Do you mean this time? Hmm, I don't know, I guess file a lawsuit, maybe against James Cameron!

* * *

The last day I worked that week was Saturday, an 11-hour shift. That was a very memorable day for me. Maybe the reason that I remember the entire day so perfectly was because of my first passenger. She was a kid with Down syndrome, a beautiful angel who got in my car with her aunt. When I gave her a piece of candy, her smile really melted my heart. Her aunt told her to thank me. She said, *"Thanks for what you've done today!"*

To me, that sentence seemed a little strange and unconventional which occupied my mind for the whole day.

I asked myself: *"What have I done? Today? In my life? I did nothing!"*

Right after that ride, I had an Uber pool ride with three different accounts and four riders: a very nice girl, a handsome Navy sailor and finally an old couple.

The girl and the sailor, who was a real gentleman, sat next to each other in the back seat. I don't like to talk about love at first sight, but it was very clear to me, to the old couple, and even to the girl, that the young sailor wanted to say something to her. It was obvious that the girl liked to hear it from him, but for some reason the young man could not express it.

I drove slowly, but the closer we got to the girl's destination, the more anxious we all got.

Finally, a minute before reaching the girl's destination, the old lady spoke up.

Old lady: Could you please have a short stop at this store?

Me: Ma'am, this is Uber pool ... I'm sorry but I'm not allowed ... I mean it's okay with me, but other riders' time is important.

Young girl: Actually, it's okay with me.

[I looked to that sailor with a big smile.]

Me: Sir, is it okay if I stop here for just a little?

Sailor: Oh yes, please do it!

[Everyone laughed, then I stopped at the store and looked at the old lady.]

Me: Here you are, Ma'am.

Old lady: James, can you go and buy a bottle of wine?

Old man: What? Why me?

Old lady: Oh, James! [Everyone laughed again!]

Old man: I mean, this store may not have ...

Sailor: [to the young girl] *You are very close to your place. Would you like to take a walk with me so these nice people can go to another store?*

Young girl: Hmmm…fine!

Old man: Good job, boy! [Everybody laughed again, then the young girl and the sailor left the car, but just before leaving he came up to me.]

Sailor: Thank you, man. Keep the meter running until my destination and you will get a hundred percent tip as well!

When they left, I tapped the young lady's trip to indicate a completed trip, and then I found out the sailor was going to walk another six miles! When I said that to the old couple, we all laughed for a minute. Then I asked the couple if they really needed the wine. James told me: *You will get a good tip, but no thanks, we don't need wine."*

After that trip, I was still thinking about what the little girl with Down syndrome had told me. *What I have done,* not today, but in my life.

That afternoon I had a ride request from a beach that was very far from my home, and I didn't realize how gradually I got there. Two couples entered my car in very stylish clothes, barefoot with shoes in hands, drunk and in a great mood. The ride was a short drive to a nearby hotel. They were laughing non-stop. The account holder told me that they were at an awesome wedding party, which was held at the beach, with the greatest food that he had ever had in his life. When we got to their hotel, if I hadn't reminded him, he would have forgotten his shoes. He was very grateful that I reminded him. He mentioned that losing those shoes would have cost him about $600 and ruined his day completely.

Immediately after that ride, I had another request from that same beach again! This time, I picked up the bride and groom!

Me: Congratulations, I just dropped some of your guests in front of a hotel, which is two miles from here.

Groom: Thank you, thank you, and we are going to the same hotel, too.

Me: You know, your guests were very happy and satisfied. They told me that this was the best wedding party they had ever had.

Bride: Thanks for saying that. So happy to hear it.

Me: No, I should say thank you because it's the first time I have a bride and groom in my car, and this nice ride will be in my memory forever. By the way, besides being a driver, I'm also a photographer. This is my business card, and I would love to give you a free photo shoot session as a gift!

Groom: Oh, thanks a lot. Buddy, you already made our day by relaying the nice things from our guests. I wish I could accept the gift, but we don't live here, and tomorrow we will go back home. If you would like, let's take a selfie together, and I will send it to you.

I gladly accepted it and took a selfie with his phone. When we arrived, they got out in front of a bar next to the hotel. He took my business card to email that selfie, but unfortunately, he forgot to send it to me.

[Months later, I picked up another bride and groom, these lovely and kind hearts, Gerald and Missy. I told them this story, and they suggested I take a selfie with them right then, which I did.]

* * *

Later that night, my last ride was for a pregnant woman with a small travel bag. At the pick-up point, I went out to help her carry her bag. She thanked me a lot for that, the bag wasn't heavy at all.

During the trip, I wondered where she was going this late. Her destination wasn't close to the airport or Amtrak. I was new with the app, so I didn't know how to figure out if the address was a house, hotel, or even a station. I didn't ask her because I didn't want to disturb her peace. I guess she noticed what I was thinking so she told me:

Pregnant lady: Tonight, hopefully, I'm going to deliver.

Me: What? What do you deliver?

Pregnant lady: A baby!

Me: Hah?!!!

For a short moment, we stared at each other, then we both realized my funny mistake and laughed out loud. She told me her husband was in the navy, she was home alone. So, just to be on the safe side, she preferred to go to the hospital now, the day before her delivery date.

During that trip, I tried to drive very smoothly, and she noticed. When we arrived, I helped her with her bag again, and she told me: *"You are a gentleman. …Well done …and God bless you!"*

Well done? … Done? … What have I done? … On my way home, I was still thinking about it and about my entire day.

I saw three stages of life, the beginning of a relationship, then newlyweds and finally an impending birth.

When I next spoke with Mehrdad, he told me he appreciated my stories!

Mehrdad: Man, I know you're just trying to reduce my stress, but the stories are really interesting. How do you make up those stories? I mean, you should write them …

Me: WTF! I'm telling you the truth…believe me, today I had a kid like Golshomar in my car, she was thankful for what I have done! I only gave her a piece of candy! It was a very small thing to do to make a person happy. I mean, of course I did it with my heart because she reminded me of our dear Golshomar but … anyway, after hearing her words, many small things made my day more beautiful. I know that sounds crazy, but all the stories were real. Those things really happened to me! Look, I made almost $100 in tips.

Mehrdad: Did the kid give you a tip?

Me: No but she revealed a way!

Mehrdad: Huh?

Me: Golshomar showed me a way!

I felt that Golshomar showed me a way to fulfill my life!

* * *

People may think that I'm a weird person, but I want to mention that the pleasure I got from driving Uber and Lyft on that weekend was better than a trip on a cruise ship. Also, I made $1,602, which was more than my weekly income from my photography job.

However, the most important thing that I had done that week was make a decision. I decided to write these stories in a book. I decided to do something with my life. I wanted to write a book and hopefully from the proceeds help some children with Down syndrome to live longer and happier.

For the happiness of all the Golshomars out there.

That day, I decided to drive for both rideshare companies as much as I can, provide the best service, and help people with little favors. They may be small actions and small steps, but I always do them with all my heart. I want to become a different driver, a driver who writes stories for the benefit of the children. From that day on, I started working for Uber and Lyft seriously. I set some goals for myself. I became a new person. I call myself a "Goodwill Rideshare Driver," a weird driver with a funny mustache who drives during all his free time so he could meet the people who would inspire these stories.

A rideshare writer was born.

Tip Pages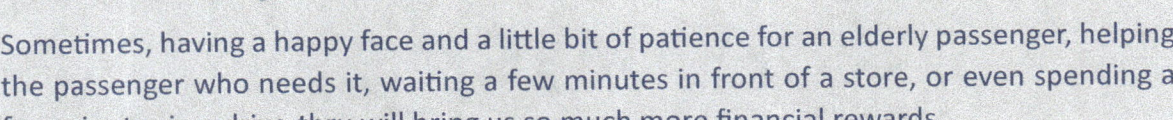

Sometimes, having a happy face and a little bit of patience for an elderly passenger, helping the passenger who needs it, waiting a few minutes in front of a store, or even spending a few minutes in a drive-thru will bring us so much more financial rewards.

Believe it: Kindness will bring you more spiritual and financial benefits than the possible money that you can make extra on the peak demand and surge* time.

When you drop off a solo passenger in front of an Airbnb, tell her or him that you will wait there for two minutes so that the passenger can go and check to see if everything is okay. Do this without expectations, but just look at that person's grateful face and reap the upcoming fruit of your kindness tree.

In other words, what goes around, comes around. If you have not tried this yet, try it one day. If it doesn't work, you can always go back to your daily routine.

*Surge: Sometimes Uber raises prices due to increased demand for rides. It's called a surge.

CHAPTER 5

The Police!

I started this job as a challenge. Aside from what I wanted to do for children, I set two main goals for myself. First, to drive 100,000 miles in this job and second, to become a very good driver. In about a year and a couple of months, I drove 100,000 miles, and even a few weeks before that, I had made 100,000 dollars. I remember before immigrating, I had to attend a class on living in the U.S. and the American culture. One day in that class, the teacher told a funny fact: He said, "Guys, do you know what the first problem that immigrants will face? Being pulled over by the police because of a driving violation."

I saved some points from that class in my mind but even with the training I received in that class, as I said before, I was still a terrible driver when I came to the U.S.

I passed the driving test on my first attempt, and I got my driving license in the very first month. I had driven in the United States for seven years with a clean driving record and I never once was stopped by the police. My average speed during those years was something around 85 mph.

Do you think I'm lucky? For several months during the time period of that driving challenge, I was learning every day, but for a while I still was a bad driver. I miraculously never encountered the police. I maintained a clean driving record, no getting pulled over, no ticket, nothing... nothing until one night, the night that I got pulled over by the police three times in a row!!!

That night, there was a music festival in San Diego. The first time that I got stopped I had four young men in my car, all of whom were drunk. As I drove, the traffic speed suddenly dropped. The cars lined up behind a stop sign.

I didn't know what was going on. I saw a police officer standing next to the stop sign, looking at the drivers' faces and randomly sending some of them into a nearby parking lot.

My Uber/Lyft sticker was on a tiny vinyl sheet leaning against the corner of my windshield. It was easy to put on or take off. It was a little loose that day, so it looked like someone hastily tried to install it temporarily. The ride was a short one, and the drop off point was two minutes away from the point we were.

Right before us, the officer allowed four cars to pass, but when I got to the stop sign, he looked at my face then he looked to the tiny Uber/Lyft sticker and said:

" You! Turn right into the parking lot. It's a DUI checkpoint!"

When we turned into the parking lot and came to a stop sign, another officer approached and asked:

Officer: Did you drink any alcohol, or do you have any open alcoholic beverage containers in your car?

Me: I'm an Uber, sir. I'm one of those boring people who almost do not smoke and drink at all!

Officer: Almost? Almost at all?! Hmmm...hmmm… Okay!!!

[The young riders tried not to laugh, but they were almost exploding especially because of my confused face and the smell of alcohol inside the car.]

Me: I'm Uber Sir! Officer: Huuuum!

The officer had some flyers in his hand, but one of them fell on the ground, so he bent over and picked it up with his thumb and index finger, then …

I guess, without any purpose, he put his middle finger in my face. and told me:

Officer: Hmmm, okay. Look at my finger. Keep your head steady and follow my finger with your eyes.

Me: This finger, sir?! Really…

We passed the checkpoint, but the drunken riders were laughing non-stop until we got to the destination. The account holder added a $20 tip to the ride and told me he will never forget my face! Maybe because I was the first driver he knew who saw the middle finger of a police officer on duty!

* * *

A few hours later, I wanted to go back to the music festival venue to pick up a few. The police had already closed one of the streets to that place, the street that was open a few hours before.

When I got to that intersection, all the traffic lights were flashing red, which means the same as a stop sign. The left turn was closed, and I didn't see it, so I went to the left lane, and immediately a police car came right behind me.

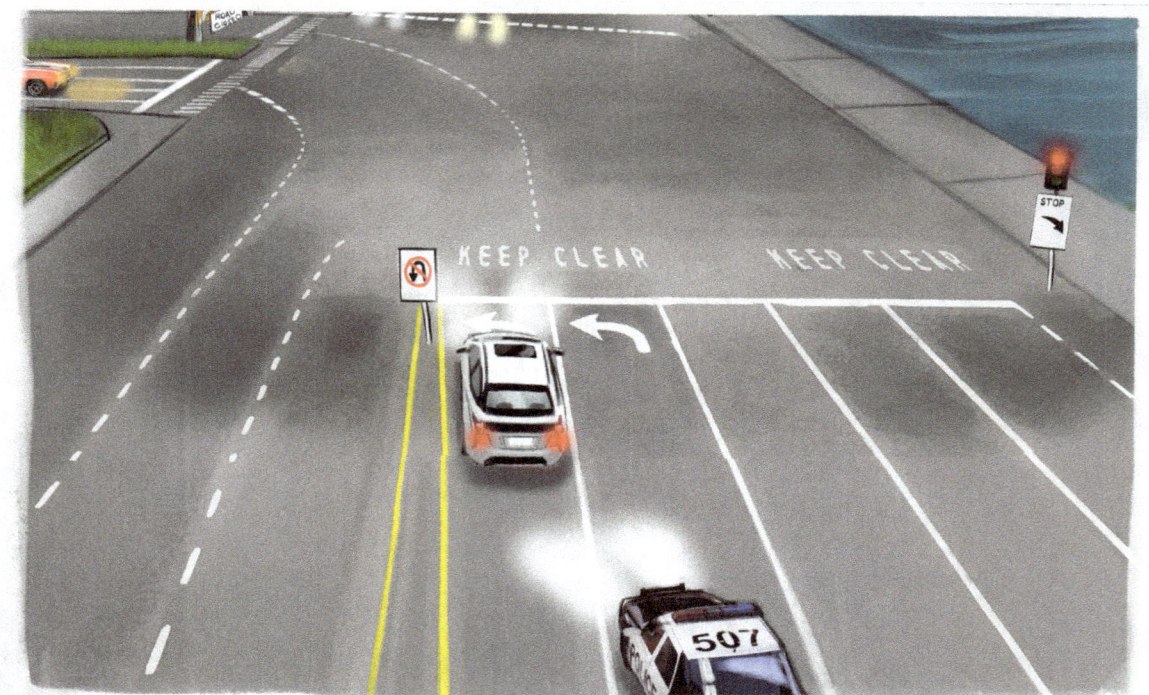

I saw the police car in my rear-view mirror, then I saw the left turn was closed, and there was no U-turn allowed.

"Oh shooot!"

That situation froze me for a few seconds, but it was my turn to go, so all the cars at the intersection waited for my move. I needed to think fast, so I thought to myself, *"Okay, okay, I can't make a U-turn because it's terribly wrong and turning to the left is not possible. What should I do? If I make any move, I will get a ticket, so I will not move at all. At least, I can say that I haven't done anything wrong."*

I wanted to turn off my car right there and maybe claim my car broke down.

I waved my hand to other drivers, begging them to move.

I was about to turn my engine off when the police officer turned his light on and said over the loudspeaker, *"Go to the gas station!"*

I turned left and went into the gas station. He followed me in that direction but entered into the street from the corner of the barrier. He looked at me with a serious frown, passed my car, and left.

It was the most beautiful frown I had ever seen in my life.

I whispered under my breath, *"Oh my dear, please go! It's okay. Even if you show me another middle finger, but just go!*

When I left that gas station, I thought that it was the worst and the longest heart-stopping moment that I would experience today or for a long time. Surely, I would not experience anything harder than those 15 seconds, at least for a while. *"Up to now, I had seen a police officer's middle finger and another officer's frown. What else can happen?"*

* * *

Let me tell you something, when you wonder what else can happen, you are booking another problem for yourself, and it's definitely bigger than the last one!

I remember it was a Saturday night, and for my Saturdays I had set a goal to find at least one story for my book and to earn at least $250. [I should mention that $250 was almost a good goal at that time.]

It was after 3 a.m. and I already had two stories featuring cops. I did not want any more stories of that sort, but until that moment I had earned $249. I have a little OCD*, which means I am one of those people who mentally needs to finish something, so I really wanted to earn one more buck before going home...

...I was tired and still a little shocked from the two previous cop encounters, so I said to myself, *"Okay, I'm going home, but on the way, if I get a ride request, I'll accept it to make that remaining dollar."*

---

*   *OCD: Obsessive-Compulsive Disorder*

I remember driving in an almost empty street. There was just my car and a black car that was a little farther behind me. I had to make another damn left turn to get onto the highway and drive toward my home. I knew if I got on the highway, I probably wouldn't get any other ride requests. Honestly, I was still thinking about that one dollar, so I slowed down and looked at the app.

I was close to a full stop in the left lane when the traffic light turned yellow. The black car passed me and exactly at the same time a ride request popped up on my phone. To make that one dollar, I immediately accepted that ride. Because the ride request was from the downtown area, I had to quickly get out of the left lane and go straight. After doing that, the traffic light changed to red. That was when I noticed the black car was a police car. OMG!

When I changed lanes, the police car immediately stopped on the other side of the intersection. He had seen my maneuver in his mirror, and now it looked like he wanted to wait for the traffic light to turn green so when I passed by him, he could pull me over and give me a ticket.

*Ohhhh F*********k!* A few hours ago, I was thinking that I had endured the most stressful 15 seconds of my day. Now, I had 60 seconds of pure stress in front of me. I wanted to make a buck, but now he was probably going to give me a $250 ticket. *"Ohhh F***************k!"*

I thought to myself that if I turned left and tried to enter the highway, this story would most likely end up with police handcuffs around my wrists. If I went straight, I would definitely get pulled over. What if I stopped here, after the green light? But I had a rider waiting for me, I wanted to make one dolla... *"Oh shut uuup stupid!!"...* [I was talking loudly and nervously to myself.]

*Me: ... Shut up, stupid! Do you still want that F***ing dollar? No... No ... But what the hell should I do? Think, think, THINK! ... He saw me, yes, he did! Oh, GREEN! Ooooh...*

Think, Thiiiiink, THIIIIINK

When the traffic signal turned green, something came to mind, something that I had learned in that "culture class"!

I approached him very slowly, maybe at less than 5 mph. He was watching me in his side mirror. When I got next to his car, I turned my hazard lights on and pulled over in front of him. It was a very stressful decision, but I did it myself! I got my driving license, registration, and proof of insurance ready and waited for him. He turned his lights on and came to me with a big smile on his face.

Officer: *Registra...*

Me: *All is here, … here you are, sir.*

Officer: *Do you know why I pulled you over?*

Me: *I pulled over myself, sir! Yes, sir.*

He looked at my miserable face, and I bet he was trying very hard not to laugh. My face looked like that of a crying child who knows his mistake, regrets it, and hopes that a painful punishment does not await him.

Officer: Say it.

Me: I changed my lane at the last second with a dangerous maneuver, but I saw ...

Officer: This excuse doesn't help you!

Me: Yes, sir, I am not making any excuses, I know it's my fault I know even yesterday around 10 p.m. somebody had an accident here just for the same reason... You asked me why I changed my lane... because I got a call from downtown and maybe right now a drunken rider is waiting for me and if I don't pick him up, he may drive drunk.

Officer: Does this reason allow you to commit traffic violations?

Me: No, sir, I told you... You are a hundred percent right, I don't have any excuse, it's just that I saw my app and I did it... maybe by picking up that person I would avoid a possible accident.

Officer: Avoid a possible accident, ha? [He had a big smile on face]

Me: I'm a good driver, sir, with a clean record...

Officer: And you committed a violation! [He looked at the DUI flyer on the front of my dashboard from the DUI checkpoint.]

Officer: You have been in a DUI checkpoint today, hah?

Me: [with a tear in my eye] *Humm...*

Officer: Is your rider still waiting for you, or did he cancel it?

Me: Still waiting ...

Officer: Okay, I won't give you a ticket this time, but I hope you learned something...

Me: Humm ... I did.

When I left him, the officer drove behind me. A mile farther down the road, two drunken riders next to a boat sat on the curb waiting for me. While I picked them up, the officer passed me. I told them how sorry I was for being late. I thanked them for not cancelling the ride, and then I explained the whole story to them. They laughed a lot when they heard that I pulled myself over. They told me they couldn't cancel the ride because it was too late, and they might get charged the $5 cancellation fee. They gave me that money as a tip even though I was late by at least 15 minutes. They said they enjoyed that funny story!

That tip gave me an idea. On the following week, I tried an idea! I was telling this story to many of my passengers like an "open mic" comedy show and I made $249 tip on the trips that I had the opportunity to tell that story! I remember the amount of the tips exactly because it was one buck less than $250!

Tip Pages 💡

Regardless of how much driving experience you have, how lucky you are, or how many years you've gone without getting a ticket, if you keep doing the wrong thing, you will eventually get caught!

By default, no police officer will stop a driver without a reason. A police officer is almost always right, and even if you think the police officer is wrong, you don't need to say that to him. Whether or not you're right, never argue with a police officer.

Please do not misunderstand me. This is not a piece of advice to make you a better driver. This is an advice that may increase your chances of escaping from hell without getting fined!

Some helpful key sentences that may help in conversation with police officers are:

You are right.

I just tried to avoid an accident. (Use only if it is true.)

I learned my lesson.

CHAPTER 6

DUI Disease!

When I was in high school, my friend Dara faced some kind of educational ban and other restrictions, so he and his family immigrated to the United States. He was a smart guy and, as I heard from another friend, these days he runs a very successful business in Orange County. We were close friends, and whenever he was in trouble, he would call me for advice and sympathy.

He came to the U.S. years before me. I was still in Iran, and we were living about twelve time zones apart, so for a while we didn't have any phone conversations. Those years, my family lived in a house with a landline phone. I remember the phone was in my father's bedroom. One night, my father angrily came to my room, woke me up and said, *"Come on, a friend of yours has called from the United States and wants to talk to you. It's 4 a.m. Oh my God!"*

That night, when I was talking to my friend, it was the very first time that I ever heard about DUI!

He used to call me Zari, a kind of funny nickname and a short form of my last name, Nozari, but it also sounds close to my religion, Zoroastrianism. We both had different religions from the majority of the students, and it was our cool link.

Dara: Hey, Zari, I got a DUI …

Me: Dude, it's 4 a.m. here!

*Dara: I know, but I am F****** up!*

Me: What's DUI? Is it a virus like HIV? You got AIDS?

[He almost was crying.]

Dara: I have ruined my life, oooh, I did s**t in my life. My father is very angry.

Me: My father, too! Okay, calm down. You did what? What do you mean…Diarrhea?

Dara: Oh, come on! I did s**t all over my life for at least a year!

When he calmed down, he explained to me that he and his friend secretly drank some alcoholic beverages without informing their families. They were drinking inside a parked car while the engine was on because they wanted to use the car's stereo to listen to music, but they weren't going to drive the car at all.

Anyway, unfortunately I didn't know what I could say to help him or even to calm him down that morning. After that conversation, I didn't hear anything from Dara for many years, and I didn't even know what happened to his DUI case. But that was the day I found out that "Driving Under the Influence" which they called "DUI" is a very serious problem in the U.S. It can ruin your life for a year or more.

As a kid I found out it is like a disease and like diarrhea it gets s**t all over a person's life!

I know it's 4:30 a.m. but he had a dangerous type of diarrhea and was making out a will!

* * *

The second time that I saw someone crying because of this disaster was when I had a drunk passenger.

I remember that the passenger was so drunk. He had a five-dollar bill in his hand as he took the front seat. He kept looking at that five-dollar bill, then he almost started crying! I was shocked. I know this is very unusual, but believe me I do not make this up, those are weird stories that really happened to me in the more than 7000 trips I had made. Anyway, he pointed to a truck and said:

*Drunk: Take this f***ing 5 bucks... fare... here... Take it and stop near that truck!!*

Me: Sir, you don't need to pay any cash. The app will take it from your submitted debit or credit card.

*Drunk: I know... take it... This f*** 5$ ruined my life... take it and stop there pleassssse.* [I stopped next to a pickup truck that was parked in the street in front of a bar. He went and took something from his truck, locked it and came back to my car.]

*Drunk: Okay, now go to my f***ing house.*

Me: Okay! But you don't need to pay $5 for that short stop... However, your account will get charged something around 25 cents each minute and you have already paid for...

*Drunk: I f****ing know it ... this is for you ... OKAY!?*

Me: Sure, thank you, I have a super cold-water bottle here. Please help yourself, and if you don't mind, I'd really like to know why do you want to give me this extra money?

Drunk: This is my favorite bar for spending time on the weekends. My house is just two miles away from here. Almost every weekend, I used to drive to this bar with a friend of mine, having a good time with her and drinking together. I used to give her a ride to the bar, then we would leave the truck here, take a $5 ride home and have a fun night there as well. The next morning, she would give me a ride back in her car to pick up my truck. One night, she went to her colleague's party, and she didn't come with me.

Me: O...oh!!

*Drunk: I wanted to order a ride, but it was a f****ing surge* so I needed to pay $10 for the usual $5 ride ...*

Me: Oh noooo!

---

*   Surge: Sometimes Uber raises prices due to increased demand for rides. It's called a surge.

Drunk: I felt that I don't want to pay double for such a short ride, plus another ride next morning to pick up the truck, then I thought, come oooon it's just two miles, and I can even walk, but I'll drive, and nothing is going to happen!!

Me: You got pulled over?

Drunk: At the first mile! That cop was following me from here!

Me: Oh God ...

Drunk: This f***ing $5 costs me over $15,000 plus my job and my girl! ... This is a punishment that every week I force myself to pay an extra five dollars!

THE COST OF DRIVING UNDER THE INFLUENCE.

The Cost In America.

DUI costs the United States (US) $114,300,000,000 every year (114.3 Billion).

Over 10,000 people die every year in DUI related collisions on our nation's roadways.

Alcohol is a factor in 31% of US traffic fatalities.

The average driver is four (4) times more likely to be involved in a fatal alcohol related crash at night than during the day.

On an average, 1 alcohol-impaired-driving fatality occurs every 51 minutes.

Personal Impact

Once arrested for DUI in California you will face the loss of your driving privileges, as well having your car impounded and driving record affected for the next ten years.

Cost of a first time DUI: $15,649

Costs include bail to get out of jail, vehicle impound and storage fees, court fine and associated fees, an increase in your vehicle insurance, attorney's fees, the cost of getting your license back, and attendance at the MADD Victim Impact Panel Class.

Sources:
The National Highway Traffic Safety Administration "Traffic Safety Fact—"December 2013"
Automobile Club of Southern California "LA Times article March 14 2013"

PW/PS-157

This flyer was given to me by a policeman the day the story of chapter 5 happened. The cost of driving under the influence by the time you read this is much higher than what is mentioned!

* * *

Two weeks after that trip, I had a lady passenger named Tania from the same bar. Because I had a story from that bar, I saw the opportunity to start a conversation, so after my regular greeting and offering a bottle of cold water, I began to tell her the story of that drunk man. She wasn't surprised; the real surprise was her story.

Tania: I had the same story here…

Me: What?!

Tania: Yes, and I almost cried … even more!

Me: What do you mean even more?

Tania: It was my birthday and two of my friends asked me to go to that parking lot, and I was thinking that we'll go somewhere else from there, but many of my friends were there and they surprised me in front of that bar. We had a good night, and I only ordered one glass of wine. I thought the amount of alcohol in my system was not high, so I decided to drive back home, and I was sure no one would even suspect me.

Me: Oh no …

Tania: In front of the bar after I put the gifts and balloons in my trunk. As I turned on the engine and started driving, I saw a police car on the corner…

Tania: …The officer looked at me, and it was too late to change my decision, so I started driving back home, which was three miles away from the bar.

Me: You got pulled over?

Tania: No, thank God. But believe it or not, that police car, without pulling me over, followed my car all the way to my apartment's parking lot!

That night, before getting to my car, I needed to use the restroom, but I postponed it until I got home. When he started following me, I urinated in my car due to severe anxiety. He didn't pull me over, but I really found out that it wasn't worth it at all. I learned my lesson on my birthday that my peace of mind is worth way more than the money that I would spend on Uber or Lyft!

CHAPTER 7

The Three Times I got Scared!

During this driving challenge, I made over seven thousand trips and almost all the trips were safe with no reason to be scared. One day I read somewhere that humans instinctively run away from facing fear. Reading this sentence had occupied my mind for many hours. A question had arisen in my mind.

Running away, fears, if running away from fears is part of our nature so is it okay to run away?

I was thinking about this job, some people have that feeling that driving in the rideshare business might be intimidating. They don't want to try it because they don't want to face any unknown fear. That is understandable! Somehow before starting this job, I was feeling the same. A higher power threw me into this pool. I had to swim. I decided to start this driving challenge, but I was still afraid. I didn't have an answer to my question, and it wasn't okay!

I remember one night in the middle of the week. I woke from a nightmare about death. I live alone in the United States and unfortunately my family is not with me. After that nightmare, no matter how much I tried to sleep, I couldn't. It was about 3 a.m., so I said,

"I would go out and drive a little, and if there was a trip request, I would accept it, and if there wasn't any requests, I would drive on the highway and listen to music. Hopefully, that would help me feel better."

I took four bottles of cold water and my photography equipment so I could go to my 7 a.m. photo shoot after some driving. I left my home and started driving and listening to light music.

While driving, I received a trip request which the account's name was something similar to Deer or Dear. Because I accepted the request so fast, I didn't see the name clearly, and I didn't care enough to look again. I didn't even care about how far away the pick-up location was. I just wanted to spend some time and keep my mind busy with the passenger's name to forget that nightmare. Anyway, I felt relaxed driving at night.

On my way to pick up the passenger, I imagined what a person named Deer or Dear would look like. Hopefully, she would be a beautiful and talkative girl with nice things to say who could make me forget about my nightmare about death.

When I got to the pick-up point, what I saw ruined my fantasy.

I saw a 6-foot-7 man, with at least 30 inches of shoulder width, who had a hoodie and something like a cracked apron on top of it. He opened the front door and sat next to me. I asked him:

Me: What's the account name, sir?

Dear: My name is Dear.

Me: Your name!? Oh ...

Dear: Oh...?? [I got it I shouldn't say "oh" so, I tried to greet him warmly]

Me: Oh nice! Please feel free to adjust your seat, make it more comfortable... this is a very cold water. Please feel free to serve yourself.

Dear: Really? Oh, thank you. You're a nice person.

Me: You're welcome, sir.

Dear: You always work around this time?

Me: Yes and no! I work mostly on the weekends, and I love to work late, but during the week I don't work as a rideshare driver because of my daytime job, I wish I could...

Dear: Why do you wish it?

The trip was about 30 miles long, and the man, although he sounded kind and polite, had a huge body which, subconsciously, was a little frightening to me. He made me nervous. The other weird feeling I had was that when Dear took the front seat, for no reason I felt that another person got in the back seat at the same time he closed the door. I heard something like the back door being slammed. I even turned back three or four times to make sure that nobody was there. There was nothing but I still felt like someone was sitting in the back seat!

He asked me why I wished it... I had to answer his question, and it would have been better to start a conversation that diverted my mind from the weird feeling and fear.

Me: Why do I wish? You know... working at night is very exciting... some people may get scared to work at night, but not me! I know there is no reason to be afraid because I have two cameras in my car and company tracking every second of all the trips, so there is no reason to be scared... No, no, I am not afraid at all. I like to work at night because I wish I could collect some scary stories for my screenplay and my book. ... Did I say I am not afraid at all? Oh no, I am not!

Dear: Haha... My job is full of scary stories. I am a Surgeon ...

Me: Surgeon ... Scary stories at hospital?!?

Dear: Police department, coroner ... This cold water really saved me ... I'm just done with my job. I had a dead body for autopsy, I spent hours working on it... no time to drink water...

Me: Whaaaat?!! Really, dude?

Dear: What?

Me: I mean, no water to drink? Oh …

Dear: Yes. I was super thirsty!

Me: …no … water… oh… scary.

Dear: Would you like to hear some of my scary stories?

Me: Oh no! I mea… I mean… first drink your water, it may get warm!

Dear: To appreciate this cool water, I'd like to tell you all my scary stories, so you can collect them and enjoy.

Me: Oh DEAR!

Dear: One night, I was dissecting a corpse whose body had been torn apart. We suspected murder. During the autopsy, I was feeling some movement behind my head …

Me: Huaaaan … Did I say that I am not afraid at …ummmm … all?

[I turned around for a second and looked at the back seat, tears were gathering in my eyes from the intensity of the horror, but Dear was telling it with a complete coolness.]

Dear: Man, I am not afraid, either, but sometimes I really feel something like a ghost around me. Even tonight…

Me: Oh DEAR, just drink…

Dear: What?

Me: I mean, would you like another bottle of water?

Dear: No… Let me finish. … Tonight, the corpse's face turned white like chalk, and I saw …

Me: Oh De... We... We are almost there...

Dear: You still have 10 more miles to drive. Be happy I'm gonna tell you at least two more stories.

That night I really came to the conclusion that sometimes it is better to stay and face our nightmares to relax!

* * *

Many of you probably have heard the saying that the rich people build palaces in the clouds. Of course, we read in childhood stories that the castle of "Jack and the Beanstalk" is in the clouds as well!

The second trip in which I got scared to death happened on a foggy night. That was a Friday night, and the reason I remember it is because when I was leaving my home that evening, an old lady neighbor told me, *"Hey, this is Friday the 13th. Be careful. All the evil powers are around!"*

I didn't understand what she was talking about, and I even forgot about it until around 11 p.m. when I picked up a passenger with a very strange appearance. A man in old fashioned English clothing that was common in the Victorian Era. He had a cane with a bird's skull as the handle. I had never seen anything like it before.

He got into the car, sat in the back seat, said the name of the account in a muffled voice, and pointed with his cane to start driving. I always thought those scenes only existed in movies, but when I saw that guy, I just felt, *"Oh God, this is Professor Moriarty* himself who has come out of those Sherlock Holmes movies!"*

My fear increased when I offered him a bottle of cold water and he didn't even say a word in response.

Along the way, we didn't talk at all. The route was long, toward the city heights where you could see many expensive villas.

I consider myself an educated person who doesn't believe in superstitions, and I know it's very stupid, but I am embarrassed to confess that the whole trip I was thinking about Friday the 13th. With great fear, from time to time, and from the corner of my eye, I looked at the skull in the man's hand... OMG!

We suddenly reached a gate. I looked at the app, and it surprised me because we were still a couple miles away from the destination. The gatekeeper looked at the man, and the man showed him something, but I couldn't see what it was. The gatekeeper opened the gate in a strange haste and

---

*   *Professor James Moriarty is a fictional character and criminal mastermind created by Sir Arthur Conan Doyle to be a formidable enemy for the author's fictional detective Sherlock Holmes.*

greeted him with a special respect, then he gave me an orange card and told me to drive at a very slow speed.

I've been in a lot of gated communities before, but this man's behavior seemed a little strange to me. Or, it might just be my mind creating worse scenarios by the minute.

After a few minutes of driving, we reached another gate, which looked like a palace gate. For the second and last time, I heard my mysterious passenger's voice: *"Stop here!"* he said.

I took a deep breath for a moment and thought, *"Oh good, finally we had reached our destination."* The navigation seemed a little confusing and the app information showed we still had a few more minutes to go.

The fog had almost surrounded the car. I stopped and unlocked the car's doors, waited for the man to get out, but all of a sudden, the front door opened and a man with a ridiculously tiny mustache, in a weird black uniform, jumped into the car. I was shocked, and with a muffled scream, I reacted like someone who sees a jump scare in a horror movie.

The gate opened automatically, and the uniformed man told me, *"Continue on this road!"*

I drove again for a few minutes. I couldn't believe we passed the second gate, and I was still driving. I didn't have any clue where we were going, and I couldn't even see any building, of course, because of the thick fog around us. As we were going higher up the road, it was not as foggy anymore, but it looked like we were driving in the clouds. That road made me think of Jack and the Beanstalk.

You may think that I am making up this story and this was exactly what I was thinking at that moment! I was cursing myself that even if I survived, no one would believe this! As I struggled with those crazy thoughts the black-uniformed guy said, *"We have everything ready, sir."*

*"OH MY GOD! He said they are ready! Oh F*** Friday the 13th!"*, my body was completely numb from fear, and then the navigation lost the signals and that just completed the scenario!

They were ready!

I wanted to stop and tell them that I would not drive without my navigator, so they'd have to get off here. But right before I could say anything, the man in the black uniform told me: *"Stop, we arrived."*

What I saw there could make me cry. There was another gate with a keypad to enter a code! The gate was there but I couldn't see any building behind that gate.

The boss in the back seat left the car to enter a pin code. At that moment, I told the other man, *"I'm sorry. I cannot go further. I should return now."*

He laughed at me and answered, *"You cannot go any further than this even if you would like to! We have to drop him off here. Turn around to the point that you picked me up and that will be the end of the trip."*

That guy added a $10 tip to the ride. When I completed that trip, I immediately turned the app off and looked at my cellphone, it was Saturday the 14th, 12:03 a.m. No more fog after the last gate and no more fear! I didn't even know why I was so scared during that trip. What was the reason and source of those crazy thoughts?

As I drove home, I thought this is crazy, people judge each other based on their appearance, place of residence, clothing, and because of those crazy thoughts, they create scary scenarios that may not be true.

That guy added a $10 tip to the ride…I learned something, and I said to myself, "If you don't want to get judged by your mustache, by your race, by where you live, by your job, and by your native country, you should first stop all the wrong beliefs in your mind! Let's not judge people. Sometimes there is something to think about what's behind a crazy story!

* * *

The third time that I was very scared, unlike the previous times, my passenger was not a huge man or even a man with a strange appearance! My passenger was a girl that looked like a model and an accent that I guessed might be from Russia or Belarus or another Eastern European country.

In those days, my car was new and didn't have any license plates because something was wrong with my car's title. So, I needed to change the plate number, so for a couple of weeks I didn't have any plates. Of course, later, one night I got pulled over by the police and I got a "fix it"* ticket and I immediately fixed it, but that night there was no license plate on my car. When I arrived at that pick-up point, the girl was waiting for me with a huge, muscular man.

I pulled over, turned my hazard light on, rolled my window down and waited for her reaction. She looked at my face then went around the car to check the license plate. Then she frowned and came back again to me and asked, *"Who are you looking for?"* The account name was Irina, and just before I could answer her, the man called to her, *"Hey, Irina, don't forget to call me when you arrive!"* When he said that, she looked at him.

Irina: Oh, shut up!

Me: The account's name is Irina. Are you Irina?

The Man: What's wrong, Irina?

Irina: No way that I go with him, he has no license plate, and his mustache looks dangerous! ... And you just called my name so he heard it…how can I make sure he is the right person?

Me: Excuse me! Dangerrrous? Ma'am, come here … look… there is my photo on your app, which you can see, and it confirms that I'm the right person.

Irina: Show it to me. Where is your photo?

Me: Give me your phone and I will show it to you… here you are…

Irina: This is more handsome to be yours!

Me: Whaaaat?! Okay, you can ask my name. Actually, the correct way to confirm each other is that I ask your account name then you ask my name, so we both can make sure we are on the right trip. Anyway, I'm Vasna.

Irina: This guy is Vasna, and you just saw the driver's name on my app!

Me: Okay, enough please! Ma'am, I have your destination information on my app. I let you check it because I already see my information on your app.

Irina: This phone can belong to that poor handsome driver…

Me: Oh my God! Okay, so cancel the trip, wait for another driver!

Irina: I don't cancel it because I would pay the cancellation fee!

---

* "Fix it" ticket is a kind of ticket that you can correct to get the citation dismissed. Usually "Fix it" tickets could be because of "Equipment violations" (like a broken taillight), "Car registration violations" (such as an expired registration or if you did not have it with you when the police asked you for it) etc.

The Man: Irina, darling, why are you afraid of this guy? You are fully prepared. You have everything you need, and you got trained for it! If you need, just "*Zekowhot yego" …!! [He said that word in another language]

Me: Whaaaaat? Excuse meeee? Zekoowhat?! No, no, no, I will cancel it myself. It doesn't matter that I will lose my continuous rides bonus.

Irina: Okay, wait I don't want to stand here for another ride. Let's go.

The Man: Good. See? He looks like a peaceful cat! Don't worry…

Me: Dayoos ro bebin ha! [I said that in my language, Farsi; it means look at this jerk] What does Zekowhat mean?

The Man: Hahaha! Go, go… Zekowhot yego… Hahahaha!

I love reading psychology books. I remember reading in one of them about being overly suspicious, which can be life-threatening for the person suffering from it, or even for people around that person. During the trip, Irina looked at me with great suspicion. Her glances and her every move made me very anxious, so sometimes I had to look at her in the rear-view mirror to make sure that she is not going to "Zekowhat" me!

Those days, a new exit was under construction on Interstate 5 in San Diego, near the Manchester Avenue exit, but unfortunately my navigation had not gotten any update about that new exit. I knew

---

*　Explanation: Actually, that wasn't the exact word he said, I don't know the actual word because he said that word in another language. Later I searched and I found out that could be the Russian word for "stab or stabbing."

I had to take that exit, but the thing was that I didn't know what her reaction was going to be when I did. Imagine I entered a dark and new ramp that navigation couldn't confirm. She must have thought that I kidnapped her. When I took the exit, I heard her open her bag and start to say something in her language. Oh f*** she was about to *"Zekowhat"* me!

Thank God there was a large empty space on the side of the road, so I pulled over, turned the car off and ran, shouting, "Help! Help! Help!".

Dude, sometimes running away can be a wise choice! But when you have a foot long mustache and you run away shouting, you will probably make a lot of road construction workers laugh!

We are not superheroes and that is okay!

When she saw me screaming and running away, she realized her suspicions were wrong. There was no way I was a kidnapper. Kidnappers don't run away screaming for help!

The end of the story was happy. We laughed, she learned a great lesson, and I got a great tip!

Tip Pages

Sometimes, we take the wrong exit. Personally, in such cases, I immediately look at the changes in distance and the remaining time and then, while apologizing to the passenger, I tell him that by contacting the company, I will prevent any possible additional charge. (Do this if it applies.)

As they say, to err is human... Nobody is perfect, and it doesn't matter if we make a mistake, what's important is to express to the other person that we are really sorry for it and sincerely try to make up for it.

One time, I took the wrong exit, and the rider knew immediately. I did what I suggested, and he said to me, "No worries, you don't need to contact the company for it." I got a five-star rating and even a tip!

CHAPTER 8

The Longest, Scariest Trip Ever!

I just shared the three trips in which I got scared. In the third story I even left my car and ran away, but those are nothing compared to this story! At least to me, this trip was beyond scary, and it is the craziest experience that I have ever had working this job... the very unique and longest trip I have ever had!

I remember it was a Sunday night around 11:30. I already had worked for around five hours, but I wanted to go home because I just had a successful Friday and Saturday. I decided to work just a little on Sunday night and not work Monday. That way, I'd be rested and ready for my very important photo shoot on Tuesday.

At that time, I had a diamond Uber Pro profile, I could see the entire trip information before accepting it. I'm not sure, but I think at that time, some of the trip information was only available for the diamond drivers.

When I was driving home, a trip request suddenly popped up on my phone screen. The ride was around 350 miles from San Diego in California to Phoenix in Arizona!

When I saw that request, I told myself, *"Oh, come on, not again!"*

I said "not again" because I remembered in the past, when I couldn't see the trip's length information, I had accepted a trip request from a drunk guy who by mistake put the wrong destination (wrong State and wrong city) instead of a street with the same name in San Diego. When I picked up that drunk guy and I tapped to start the trip, the estimated time was something around 11 hours. I helped the guy edit the trip, and he gave me a good tip.

This time, when I saw a drop-off point in Arizona, I thought, *"Oh, okay, another drunk person who may need cold water and a helping hand to edit his destination. Probably just like the last time, this trip is less than five miles with a very good tip, so let's go!"*

When I arrived at the pick-up point, I spotted two tall and huge men. One of them had a box in hand. They didn't seem drunk, but they and their box smelled extremely like marijuana. I thought to myself "OK, probably they are high." I got out and put their belongings in the trunk, they sat in the back seat.

Me: What's the account name, sir?

First Guy: My name is Bill, and he is Jim. It's for Bill, correct?

Me: Yes, sir, but you accidentally put the wrong destination, somewhere in Arizona. Please edit it.

Bill: No, that's correct! Buddy we are going to Arizona!

Jim: Let's go, dude! Huha!

Me: Excuse me. Whaaat?!

Bill: Phoenix! And I need to be there before 7 a.m. Let's go fast.

Me: Sir, it's 11:40 p.m., it takes six hours to get there, and today I have already driven for five hours so far. I need to go home. I'm sorry, I cannot do it. I need to cancel the trip, please leave the car.

Bill: NO! No, no, hold on. DON'T cancel it. Look, my girlfriend is in the hospital… My first kid will be born tomorrow… I need to be there.

Me: Sir, I'm sorry, I cannot do it. I can give you a ride to the airport, but not to Arizona. My car is new, I don't want to drive in the desert at midnight, and I don't know you…

[I got out of my car to give them their box, but he followed me.]

Bill: Hey, I'm not a drug dealer, we are pro basketball players. Look in the box, you can search it. I will give you $300 in tips, let's just go.

Me: Even if you pay $500, I still cannot do it, sir! You can request another ride, you will find it easily, I'm a photographer, I do Uber and Lyft for fun, but tomorrow afternoon, I need to be here to get ready for an important project on Tuesday.

Bill: Look, you cannot leave me here like that. Wait, WAIT! I need to be here in San Diego by tomorrow afternoon, too. Let's go there together and I will request you again to give us a ride back here. You will make great money and you will have fun.

Me: Sir, my app will get automatically signed off after 12 hours of working, so I cannot give you a ride back to San Diego.

Bill: Come ooonnnnn! Please do it for my baby. You can become the first driver who did this for a newborn baby!

When he said, "do it for a newborn baby," Golshomar's face came to my mind. Then I thought about this book and about the new children's center and hospital. I knew this would be the craziest thing that I'd ever done to that point. They didn't look like basketball players, but whatever! I was looking for meaning in my life … I accepted it for the babies!!

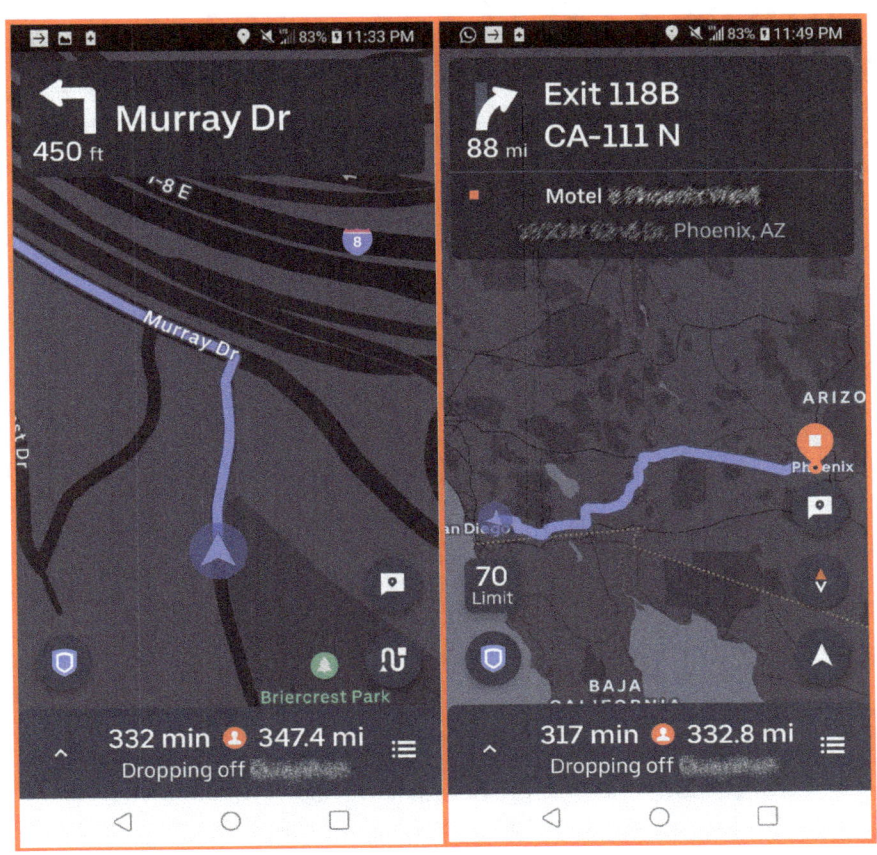

My car's gas tank capacity is listed as 11.3 gallons and averages 54.6 miles per gallon, so to be on the safe side I completely filled the tank at a gas station. In the gas station I bought snacks for everyone, and then I told them that I have two online working cameras inside my car. I also told them I set the Safety Toolkit feature to follow this trip and shared my location and trip status with my cousin, just in case he would need to call 911. I mentioned that the company monitors the trip at all times, so if we make an unusual stop, the company will ask both of us why we stopped there. They protect their drivers.

Bill gave me a mysterious, scary smile and said: *"Wait for me, I need to buy a lighter!"*

* * *

The chosen navigation route was a narrow road full of mini hills, which frequently meant going from bottom to top and back again in the middle of the desert.

The road had very strange turns and curves, even two sharp 90-degree turns. I still cannot understand why it was like that.

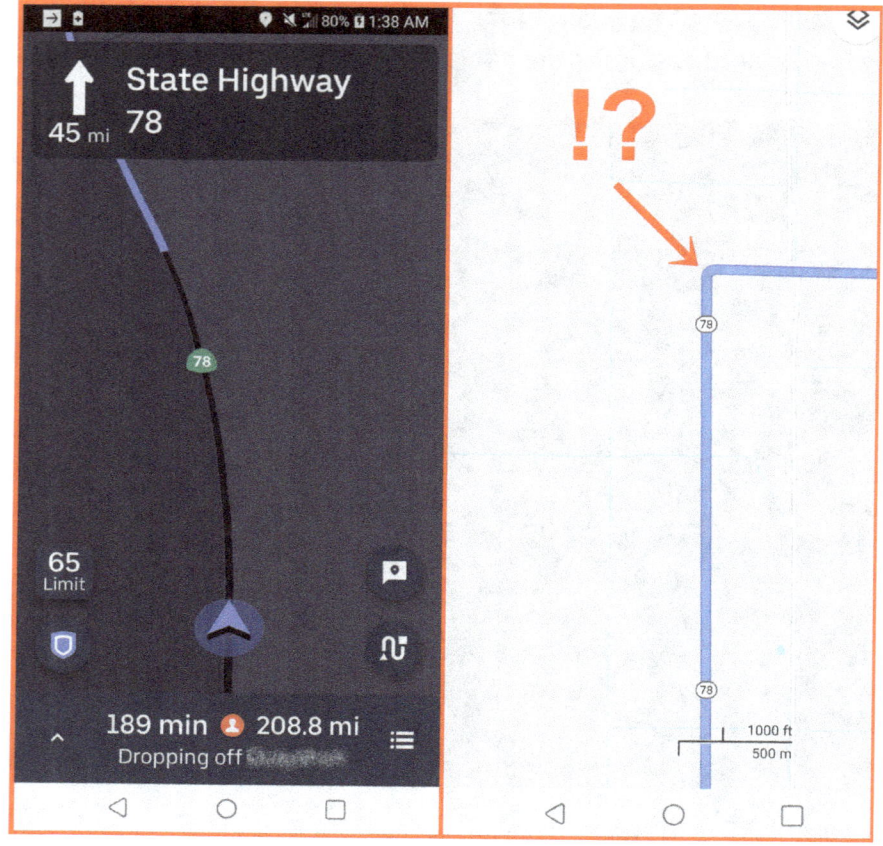

This was the first time that I had ever driven on such a road. The road itself was enough to cause the onslaught of illusory thoughts, especially because no light reflected from behind my car. The inside of the car was completely dark as well, and I couldn't see much in my rearview mirror, which made me feel unsafe. I couldn't see what they were doing, and those men were completely silent and motionless. I guessed Jim was asleep. Bill, sometimes, I could see the whites of his eyes in my rearview mirror, even though I couldn't see what exactly he was doing. One time, I turned the cabin lights on for the back seat, but it was really bothering their eyes, so I stopped.

The speed limit in many areas of that road was 35 mph, but because of many mini hills and my unfamiliarity with the road, I often couldn't drive faster than 25 mph... I remember in some parts of the road, wind had blown some thorn bushes into the road, making the road even narrower than before.

When I got close to those bushes, I slowed down as much as possible. I had to drive carefully through those bushes because I didn't want to get a flat tire.

I was thinking about going out and pushing those bushes away, but immediately I changed my mind because in the corner of the road I saw three animals, larger than coyotes. They looked like wolves!

I realized neither a flat tire nor an engine issue would make me leave the car. I passed the bushes but kept those animals in my mind for a while!

* * *

About half an hour later when I slowed to less than 15 mph to pass a sharp-looking object, maybe a piece of metal, which was in the middle of the road, I suddenly heard Bill whisper in a very muffled voice, *"Cameras!"*

I freaked out…first, I decided to turn on the cabin light immediately, but then I thought it wasn't a good idea to get on the nerves of those two huge men who stood almost 6-feet-6!

Unconsciously, different thoughts flashed through my mind. I knew that I mentioned to them about the security cameras inside my car…oh God… why does a professional athlete need a lighter? Does a professional athlete smoke? Why do they smell like marijuana? What is inside that weird, stinky box? He said "You can search it, but the box was tightly wrapped and impossible to search! If they told the truth about the baby, why is the drop-off destination a motel instead of a hospital!?

I noticed that when I slowed down, those two were making some noises. So, from that moment on, I tried to drive as fast as the speed limit. At least they would not attack me because of the risk of an accident.

The more I thought about it, the more I was convinced that they would attack me very soon.

A tear ran down from the corner of my eye. I don't know why, but in my mind, I started repeating some specific sentences of a soliloquy. It's from a masterpiece, a play that I loved and had memorized in art school.

... Whether 'tis nobler in the mind to suffer ...

... Or to take arms against a sea of troubles ...

...To die, to sleep __ No more!!

... We end the heartache and the thousand natural shocks...

... Devoutly to be wished! ...

To die, to sleep!"

I wondered why that came to my mind. I'm not making this up, those sentences kept repeating in my mind. I had no control, and my eyes filled with tears. My tears and those sentences from "Hamlet," the masterpiece of William Shakespeare helped me feel a little calmer. What an ironic scene ...To die, to sleep, ... Devoutly!

I remember in those moments sometimes I prayed, and sometimes I repeated those sentences to calm down and I still tried to drive as fast as possible on that road, even a little faster than what the speed limit would allow. The embarrassing and funny thing was that hearing any noise from the back seat could scare the crap out of me!

After driving for a while in terrifying silence, I came to one of those terrible curves, so I needed to decrease my speed and pushed the brake pedal...

When I pushed the brake pedal, all of a sudden, Bill, with a frightening scream, lunged and jumped on me! His right hand firmly gripped my right hand on the steering wheel.

I was screaming, he was yelling, and Jim started to scream as well! I pushed the brake pedal strongly and immediately with my left hand pressed the car's park button and turned my body toward Bill and pushed him back with all my power. Hitting the park button caused the car to stop with a strong jolt. That and my pushing at the same time threw Bill to the back seat.

Frightened to death, I kept screaming with all my might, tried to make very loud sounds and strange movements. Some of my sounds and movements looked like what I had seen in a martial arts movie. I wanted to look like the legendary fighter, Bruce Lee! And I hoped that would scare them and make them think that I knew martial arts.

Of course, the very special self-defense and martial arts techniques I mostly use are called "Leave the car and run", but unfortunately because I thought about the wolves, I couldn't use my secret technique! So, although in the first few seconds of the clash, I had unbuckled my seat belt and pulled the door handle to open it, I didn't open it completely. I stayed in the car, and I kept screaming and moving my claws around. All of a sudden, my hand hit the door. The door opened, and the cabin's light turned on, and I saw their faces. They were no longer screaming. They were just looking at me!

If you don't know what that is, … hmmm … we have a term that says, "Someone's balls became a bowtie under his neck out of fear!" Oh dear, I hope you never get into a "Balls bowtie" situation!

[Jim's jaw dropped and his eyes rounded, spoke to Bill]

Jim: What is he doing?

[Then Bill grabbed his forehead and said:]

Bill: Stupid, insane…

Jim: Why are you yelling?

Bill: I was asleep, and when I woke up, I saw that he was going straight into the blocks and crashing the car. I bet he was asleep. I just wanted to take the steering wheel.

Me: Ohhhh myyyyy God! I was NOT …

Jim: F*** you both stupid.

Bill turned the cabin light off, and both of those guys, without any words, went back to sleep. I closed my door, fastened my seat belt, and started to drive again. After a few minutes of driving Bill told me,

"In a few miles ahead, the main road is closed with some barriers, and you have to take the road that is parallel to the main road that looks like a tunnel. You have to cross it, and in that corridor, there are some cameras installed that would take pictures with a lot of flashing light! Don't panic, but wake me up before going into the tunnel,"

When he said that, I realized this was not his first time. He's a professional! Maybe a professional basketball player!!

I was miserable and still shaking. I wasn't a superhero. I was an ordinary person without any special power who decided to face a particular fear because of the children I loved, sacrificed comfort, and stepped on the road. I was still shaking, and I needed to calm down.

Again, I started whispering some sentences from "Hamlet…"

…"Fear of death makes us all cowards, and our natural boldness becomes weak with too much thinking. Actions that should be carried out at once get misdirected, and stop being actions at all*"

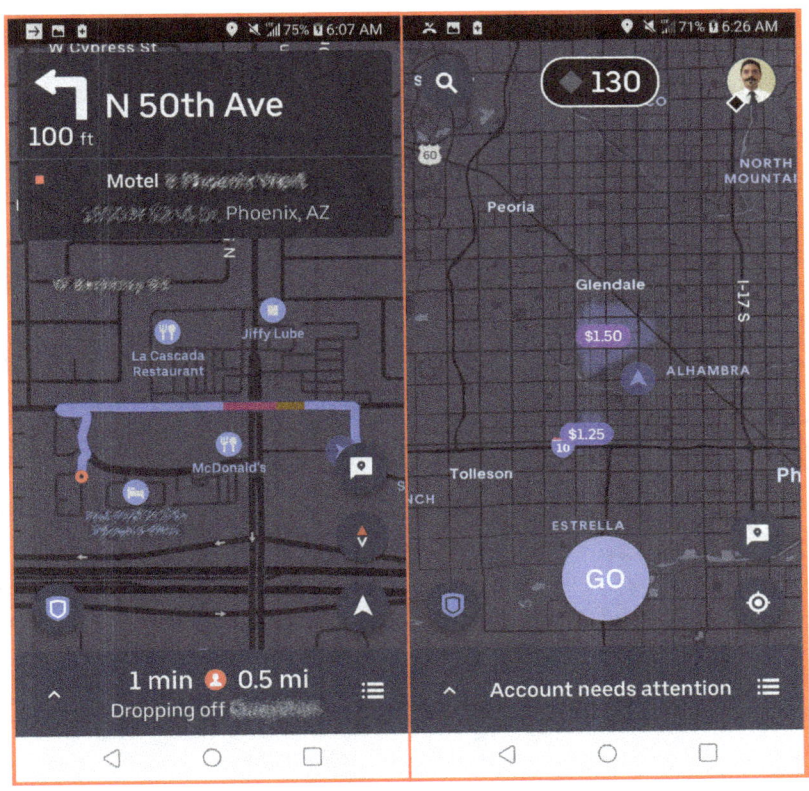

When I completed the trip, I found out that he lied about $300 in tips, he had lied about coming back to San Diego with me, and that both of my apps were "on hold" (see one of them in above picture) and I cannot use them in Arizona because they were set for California.

On the way back, it rained heavily, which made me worry about arriving on time for my Tuesday photo session, but…

I was happy! I felt like I had been guided to do something, to live a unique story… a story for my kids…

I did something, I passed a line…and …

Finally, I had something done!

---

* *These sentences come from a modern translation of that masterpiece; what I repeated during the trip was in Farsi from a Persian translation of that play.*

Tip Pages

Use the Safety Toolkit and a camera, and you most likely will be safe. You never know who's going to get into your car. An ordinary-looking person could be something you least expect, but the more prepared you are, the safer you'll be in that situation. One night, on a 26-mile trip, I told my passenger the story of that Arizona trip. Having a very humorous spirit, he laughed and said, "Dude, do you know what my job is?"

I said I did not. He said, "I am a drug dealer!"

"Oh God no!!!" I responded.

He explained that he had a marijuana plantation in Oregon, where a household can grow up to four plants on the property, regardless of how many adults live in the household. In California, the rules are somewhat different. He said selling a pound of marijuana in California is about $1,000 more than selling it in Oregon. Then he added that he did not know what was in the box of the passenger who was going to Arizona, but he could guess!

CHAPTER 9

Good Day, Bad Day

One Saturday night, I wasn't in a good mood. I didn't want to work. I didn't feel like doing anything. I didn't want to keep going... I was tired!

I was tired because I was thinking that there was no chance to build that new kids' center, I have long dreamed about driving for Uber and Lyft. I didn't feel I could write a book in English that people who were born in the U.S. would enjoy reading, or even could read! This is a crazy goal which I cannot reach....Never! On that day, I was overwhelmed... I was so down and sad.

Most Saturdays, I worked for Uber or Lyft from 6 p.m. to 6 a.m. and my goal was to find at least one story for my book and make $250.

But that day I was very disappointed and sad, so I said to myself, "I will not do this anymore. It is nonsense to take small steps, pursue small goals and hope to achieve the main goal. Today is a bad day, and the worst part about it is, no good day will come, and all my efforts will be in vain if I do not make a big move!"

That night, instead of driving, I went to bed around 6 p.m., played a little with my cellphone, listened to some music and finally tried to sleep. But that seemed impossible with my overwhelmed mind.

It was around 11 p.m. when I thought, "I can't stay at home anymore. Maybe a little driving could calm me down. I don't want to make $250, and I am not looking for any story. Just a little night driving on Interstate 5 to relax, and maybe talk a little with one or two passengers."

I took only five bottles of ice water and left the house.

I'm not exactly sure if it was the first or second ride request that I received, but I got an UberX request, and when I went to the pick-up point, two men and two women got into the car. The account holder was a gentleman who took the front seat. I said my normal start-up greeting, then offered them cold bottles of water. I always keep all types of common phone chargers in my car, and when he saw one of those chargers next to the seat, he plugged his phone into that charger, then put his phone on the floor mat. He took one of those very cold waters and started drinking it.

It seemed that he was really enjoying himself drinking that water. After finishing his water, he started telling a funny story about the differences between the meanings of the words bi*** and di**!

He gave a funny example and said: *"If you know my favorite pizza is the cheese pizza, and you know that I'm super hungry, you order a cheese pizza and you eat the whole pizza except one slice and leave just that slice for me, you are absolutely a di**. But if you know that I hate olive pizza and you order it and frequently tell me that you kept the whole pizza for me you are a bi***."*

I didn't feel good that night, but the way he explained it made everyone laugh out loud, even me! It was as if he was there to make me feel better, and he kept saying funny things. During the trip, he felt a little warm, so I told him if he'd like, he could take another bottle of water and adjust the air conditioning. When he got out of the car he told me, *"You made me happy and satisfied with your service!"* and I told him, *"You made me happy with your stories!"* He smiled, closed the door and left.

After dropping them off, I was feeling a little relaxed, so I said, *"Okay, now I can go back home."* On my way home, I thought, "Surely, I cannot write a story about olive and cheese, and I cannot make $250 in one hour, but at least I took a small step to help myself and help others feel better.

At that moment, suddenly, a strange light illuminated my car. I couldn't find the source and I was about to say, *"This is the light of God!!"* Then I saw...Oh shoot! Nooo! He has forgotten his phone on the mat, and it was flashing silently!"

I was driving on the highway and the phone was somewhere on the mat, which I couldn't reach. I missed that call, but I took the first exit and pulled into a gas station and immediately reported the lost items to Uber. After a few minutes, he called again and before I could say, I will bring it for you, he said, *"Please bring it to me and I will give you a $200 tip!"*

I told him, *"That's very nice of you, but I was about to bring it to you anyway."* I asked him to text me his exact address, so he did and again mentioned that he would give me a $200 tip!

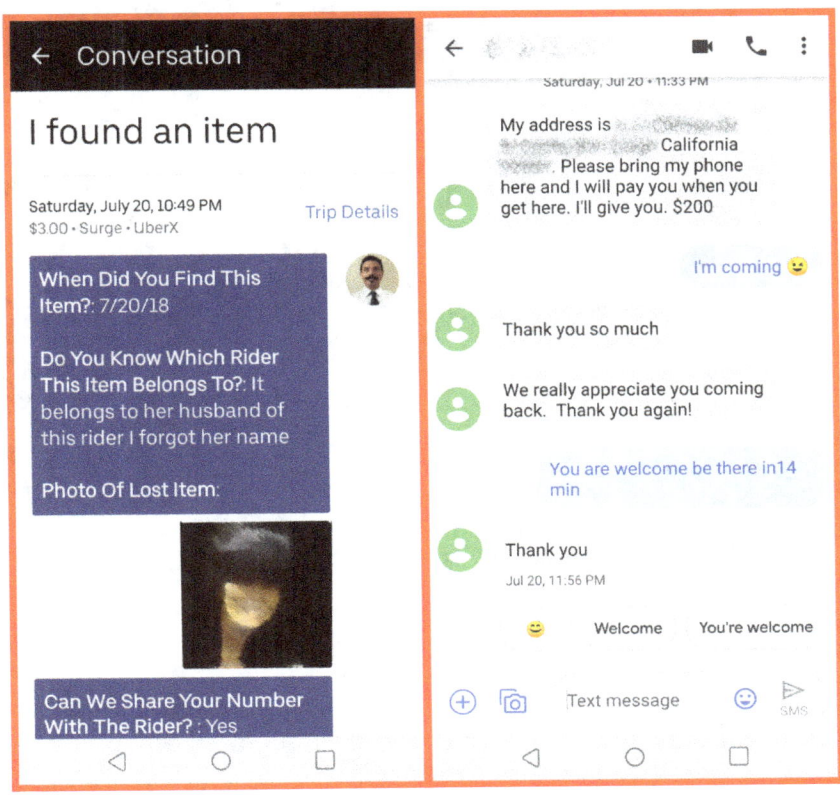

I went there and I gave his phone back to him. I couldn't believe that he gave me a $200 tip, but he did. I even asked him, *"Are you sure? It's not necessary to tip me, I had reported the phone to Uber, and I get paid $15 as a bonus for returning the lost item to a rider".* He was a real gentleman, and he said, *"I'm a man of my word, I'm happy with your service, and this is for your kids!"*

At that moment, I thought to myself, *"I am single, and I do not have kids, but this gentleman insists that the money is for kids!"* I don't know. Maybe my imagination is very strong, but that somehow warmed up my heart.

I told him, *"I would spend this money on a book, the proceeds of which goes toward helping kids! And I would like to take a selfie with you to publish it in that book, if you let me use this selfie in my book."*

He gave me a funny look, and I guess he didn't believe me, but he said, *"Okaaaaay!"*

After taking the selfie, I told him that I need to come back to get his permission and to release the photo publishing rights, but he told me, *"No worries. I gave it, I gave it."*

The ride was $3.49 but, on that trip, I made the $200 cash tip, a $5 on-app tip, a $15 returning fee plus the $3 surge on fare, for a total of $226.49! I almost made enough money for my night with a story to tell. But the most important thing to me was the weird light that I saw in my car. There is always a light for the people who want to see a light! It can be a stupid light from a cellphone, but for those who want to see, it really can brighten their way!

No matter how stupid you might think it is to believe a cellphone light is a sign, believing in something can warm up your heart!

* * *

After that trip, I wanted to go back home but I still needed $24! This time, the money itself didn't matter to me, but after what happened, I felt that I must take my little steps to reach my goal.

"I serve people for my happiness!"

There was a big surge in the downtown area, so I decided to go and serve people in that surge area! Don't laugh!

When I arrived, I turned my apps on and immediately got a trip request from downtown San Diego to Temecula. A trip of around 60 miles. When that guy got into my car, I saw that he was very sad and almost crying. I gave him a bottle of cold water and told him that if he didn't mind sharing, I'd like to know what's wrong and why does he look so sad?

He told me that he felt very stupid because he saved some money for the entire week to come downtown tonight and have some fun, but he lost his car key in the club and now needs to spend half of that money to go to Temecula and get his spare key. Then he has to pay the other half to come back here to pick up his car. He told me it was a bad day for him, and now he feels that all his efforts at a fun night have been in vain.

When he said that, I remembered how I felt two hours ago, exactly the same. Something came to my mind, so I told him, "Listen, after this trip, I'm done with my night, so when I drop you off, I will drive back to San Diego while the apps are off, and my music player is on. We can go to Temecula together, and then if you would like, I will wait for you for a few minutes. You can go and bring your spare key, then you can come back to San Diego with me for free. My home is not that far from downtown, so it's okay, I will drop you off at downtown." Then I offered him some candy from my candy box. He started to laugh and said: *"It was as if you are here to make me feel better!"*

When we arrived next to his car in downtown, he told me, *"You made me feel happy and you changed my day! How can I thank you?"*

I told him, "I didn't do anything, buddy, you don't need to thank me, but if it is okay, let me take a picture of your key."

He said, *"Okay, but why do you need it?"*

"Because this is the key to happiness!"

Tip Pages

One day, as an UberX ride passenger, I got into a very big van. Although there was enough room for my legs, the driver, who looked Asian, respectfully pushed the front seat forward to give me more room for my legs. Then he asked me if the temperature inside the car was right for me or if I would like to change it.

I said the temperature was fine. During that trip, I felt like a VIP, and although he wasn't driving smoothly, I gave him a five-star rating plus a good tip.

Later, I was thinking that I didn't need extra legroom and I didn't even adjust the temperature, but I really felt comfortable during the trip. By doing just two simple actions, he gave me the feeling that he cares about my comfort. That warmed my heart.

From that day on, as a driver, I did the same thing on all my trips. I believe I owe a large number of my good ratings to those services. Making others feel good could be a key to success, at no cost.

Care about people and they take care of you.

CHAPTER 10

Inspiration

I've learned a lot during this journey and while doing this job. It was really an amazing opportunity to meet so many people. When I interacted with them, they surprised me by showing a wide range of thoughts, beliefs, and personalities. In this job, I saw very clearly that every person has an interesting story.

Each story is enough to become a book, and each person is a live book to enjoy and learn from. I learned when we say that we can't live in this damn boring world, because we have nothing to enjoy, we have no hope for the future, and we have nothing to be thankful for, we have to think again!

Honestly, I was the person who hates those who keep saying that we have to enjoy this damn life and be thankful for it. I heard those motivational, but stupid-sounding slogans, and I couldn't relate to them enough to make me feel happy. I couldn't find a reason to be thankful for.

For more than half of my life, even before my immigration, I kept asking myself, *"What the hell am I doing in this boring and sad life?"*

I had never felt enough happiness in my life, especially after my immigration because I had to start from scratch. I was all the more lost and confused. As a result, lately I have been feeling I have even less ability to use my talent or to enjoy my life.

Sometimes you just can't understand why you are not happy enough, what are those idiots talking about when they say that nonsense about enjoying your abilities? Which ability? What do I have to enjoy hah?

I had a professor who told me, "If you don't understand something completely, you should try to describe it for another person who doesn't understand it at all!" I remember when he said it, I gave him an ugly look and I told him: *"Sir, I asked you to answer my question to make it clear for me, but this is the most irresponsible answer in my entire life!"* He laughed and I whispered obscenely and left.

* * *

Golshomar had given me a reason to do this job. Since I found a reason, these trips became a big journey for me. A journey in which I began to find a meaning for my life and find some answers.

I had three trips that really helped me find an answer to some of my questions. Somehow, I was seeking a way to the source of happiness. Honestly, at the time, I was sad and confused!

* * *

One day around 4 a.m., before going to my photography job, I looked to maybe receive a ride request. I turned my app on and immediately I got one.

My car is super silent, especially when the car uses the power of the battery. When I arrived at the pick-up point, I saw a lady standing on the other side of the street.

I thought that she must be Nikoo, my passenger, because no one else was there at 4 in the morning. I waved my hand toward her and turned the car's headlight on and off to get her attention and get her to come to this side of the street and get into the car. The pick-up point was on the right side of this narrow street, so I couldn't make a U-turn. But I couldn't get her attention!

She was a very good-looking lady, in a very colorful dress. She held a mug in her hand and was not paying any attention to me, so I said to myself, *"Maybe this lady is not my passenger. I don't want to scare and bother the wrong lady at 4 in the morning. It's better to go a little farther and make a U-turn. Maybe my rider is waiting somewhere else for me."*

When I turned around, the ride timer required me to go back to the same point, but now I was on her side. As soon as I stopped, she came toward the car, opened the front door, greeted me, and sat down in the front seat. Only when she started to walk, I saw the white cane in her hand!

I was so shocked and embarrassed because I didn't realize what the matter was, and I didn't even have a chance to get out and help her get in the car. The wonderful smell of her coffee pervaded the whole car.

I asked her: *"Ma'am what's the account name?"* She turned her head towards her phone and moved the screen up and down with her finger and said: *"Are you Vasna?"*

I was looking at her very surprised then I answered: *"Yes I am, and you are Nikoo?"* She said: *"Yes, perfect, let's go!!"*

I was completely confused, but I didn't bring it up. I told her, *"What a good aroma your coffee has. I have cold water here, but I don't think you need it."* She thanked me and asked If I have any empty cup holders.

I told her, *"Yes, here you are."*

She searched in between the seats with her left hand then placed her mug on the empty spot.

I wasn't sure what should I say. I wanted to apologize for wasting her time before picking her up, and I also wanted to apologize for not helping her get into the car. But she used her phone as if she could see and got into the car fast without any help, which made me unsure what I should say. I started driving, but I watched her from the corner of my eye very stealthily.

I saw her folded white cane next to her feet, and then her shoes got my attention. They were red with rounded toe-boxes and little scratches on top of them but waxed perfectly. Also, her clothes were noticeably colorful and tidy. I was surprised at what I was seeing, and then I got even more surprised and confused when I saw she was checking up something on Facebook and was laughing!

I couldn't control my curiosity anymore, so I asked her:

Me: Ma'am, what are you doing?

Nikoo: I'm enjoying a funny article on Facebook.

Me: Can you see it? I mean when you move the screen this fast...

Nikoo: No, I cannot see it, I'm blind! But I can hear it!

Me: What!? Hear what?! I don't hear anything...

Nikoo: My Bluetooth hands free headset is in my ear, so let me turn it off so you can hear the reading from my cellphone.

[She turned it off so I could hear an English narration, maybe 10 times faster than normal. I can't even understand things in my native Farsi at that speed. She listened and laughed.

Nikoo: Isn't it funny?

Me: I need to pull over somewhere...

Nikoo: For what?

Me: To help my dropped jaw and maybe read the text because I cannot understand what I heard.

Nikoo: Hahaha... Sorry, I need to decrease the reading speed, then you may understand it. It is set for my ability, but you may need a little help for it.

Me: Haha...Yes please.

Nikoo: Because we need to get all information by ears instead of eyes, sometimes we increase the speed of reading even up to 25 syllables per second.

Me: Really? It's even faster than what I can see, read, and understand in English!

Nikoo: Hahaha. You know, your problem starts when you mention your English. We all have abilities. We just need to stop feeling that we are unable to do things and instead look for another way to do things.

Me: And you don't need help?

Nikoo: I like to enjoy the comic texts. I cannot read them. I can ask you to help me and read it for me, but I learned how to do it by myself. I'm a teacher and I'm going to my students right now to help them learn how to use and enjoy their abilities. We just need to understand this reality and move forward, then we can help others as much as we can! First, we need to stop nagging and understand that we are able! Don't complain about a language!

Nikoo opened my eyes!

* * *

The second time that my soul was really shocked and touched was when I had four very young passengers. The oldest of them probably was around 19 years old and the youngest was perhaps 7 years old.

When I got to the pick-up point, I saw a red bus which had a large red cancer awareness ribbon on it. There were many kids getting off the bus. All the kids wore red hoodies, and it seemed they were coming back from a picnic or some gathering.

Four children came to my car. The oldest kid very politely said the account's name, and then all of them got into the car. I asked them if the temperature inside the car was okay, and I offered them bottles of water. They said everything was fine and they were not thirsty.

I wanted to do something extra for them to make them happier. So, I took out my candy box and offered them some. The youngest kid seemed to want a piece, but the oldest one said, *"Because we are fighting cancer, we help each other not to eat sugar."*

I felt stupid. That teenager seemed to understand my good intentions, and she told me that it would be great if I had an auxiliary cable in my car so they could listen to their music and enjoy the trip. I immediately attached the cable and gave it to them.

The entire trip, they were so happy. When we got to the destination and they got out of my car, the oldest thanked me and said, *"Thank you for the cable and thank you for offering candy to us. I knew why you offered it, but we've learned how to be happy without candy."*

That last sentence made me cry and made me think that I haven't learned how to be happy in my life whether I have candies or not. I learned something and I was ashamed of it for a long time!

* * *

The third time that a passenger really shocked my soul and gave me an unforgettable lesson was on a Saturday night, not long after the lessons that I got from Nikoo and those cancer-fighting heroes.

That day I had declined going to my cousin's party. He was the only close relative that I have in the U.S. After a while, he invited me to a party, but because I wanted to work on my goals, I forced myself to say no to his invitation. I was absolutely sad turning him down, especially because I was physically and emotionally tired of this effort. That night, so far, I had driven maybe less than two hours, but the pain in my knee was bothersome and I felt that the pain is because I drive a lot without giving myself enough time off.

I got a ride request from the front of a small pub. When I arrived, I saw there was a bench on the sidewalk where a handsome young man and probably his mother were sitting. A pair of crutches was leaning to the back of the bench, and a folded wheelchair was next to the mother.

I pulled over in front of the mother and pushed the front seat back to make a little more room in the front seat. I got out of the car, said hi to them, opened the front door for the lady and I said, *"Ma'am, I'll put your wheelchair in the trunk."*

As I did so, they sat in the car, but contrary to what I expected, the young man took the front seat. The mother and the crutches got placed on the back seat!

After two minutes I offered them the bottles of cold water then the young man spoke up and said:

Young Man: Today is a very good day, I'm so happy, and I'm amazed at how well everything is going!

Me: Glad to hear it.

Young Man: Thanks a lot, that you patiently put all our stuff in the trunk. I was just a little worried about them.

Me: You are very welcome, sir.

Young Man: We had a little party today, and since I recently had surgery, I'd rather have both crutches and the wheelchair. I was worried if I could fit both in a Lyft's car.

Me: I'm glad to help sir. Don't even worry about moving them when we get to your destination. I will carry all your stuff to your house. Enjoy the water.

Young Man: Vasna, I really appreciate your hospitality.

Me: You are very welcome, and I have to say you look very good after the surgery. If you don't mind sharing, what was that surgery?

Young Man: Thank you for asking that question. In fact, I was eager to explain it. I had to amputate my dearest problem makers a few days ago.

Me: Dearest!? [I felt my knee pain again, and it was ridiculous that my mind was so tired that I couldn't remember the meaning of the word "amputate," so, I asked him:]

Me: Sir, what does that mean?

The young man, using the protective cover of his cellphone, hit his prosthetic legs under his pants.

Knock! Knock!

Young Man: I have two brand new legs, and I'm so happy. I feel like I've been reborn, and I've had a chance to live, work and build a new life. I had two normal-looking legs but because of a rare genetic disease, the nerves inside my legs were tied and I endured terrible pain all my life.

Me: Ah…

Young Man: I struggled with my doctor to convince her to amputate them. Now, I have reached a point where I can work hard to build a new life without that much pain! Of course, that was a difficult decision…What do you think?

Me: You had a pain that no one knew or felt, so you made a brave decision and left a dear member behind… You made a great sacrifice to reach this point. It sounds like you have migrated from your past life to your current life! You are a dreamer's hero, and I respect you.

I forgot my pain. I forgot all my pains. I respected his efforts for a new life, I respected him!

CHAPTER 11

A Birthday For Us!

My birthday is in the last week of November. Sometimes I celebrate Thanksgiving Day and my birthday together with the only family member that I have in the U.S., a cousin, and a few friends of mine. I remember one year, we didn't have any plans, and I felt I must drive to reach my goals because they were now my beliefs and my life's dream!

It can be a little sad to work on your birthday while you help other people to get ready for their Thanksgiving parties, but I was thinking that I should do it. Sad, but it is what it is.

During my journey, especially after so many inspiring stories, I learned that helping people can bring happiness to both them and me!

Although I said I learned it, I actually knew it before that. Sometimes even when you know something, you still need to try to learn some more. When you understand how it really works in your heart, you'll feel good about it. Then your learning is complete.

When you know it without a complete understanding, that may decrease and even ruin any good feelings and beliefs you have.

...I didn't feel good...

...It could have ruined my happiness. I needed to understand it better!

I was feeling a little sad because I couldn't understand how working, even for a big goal, could make you feel happier than being at a party! It sounds like nonsense, especially when it's your own birthday party!

I remembered again what my professor had told me, *"If you don't understand something completely, you should try to describe it for another person who doesn't understand it at all!"*

I still thought it was bulls**t!

* * *

That year I worked on my birthday without any party, but at the end of the day, I didn't regret it. Something very unique and stunning happened to me, something that I later realized the seeds of it were laid years ago!

I will put a few photos and documents below these paragraphs as proof. This is a true story, even though the chances of these events happening all together and in a row are as low as the chances of winning the lottery. But guess what? Sometimes people win the lottery!

* * *

That night, on my birthday, I had a very drunk and very sad passenger. His name was Adam. When I noticed he was drunk, I offered him a bottle of water, which he took willingly and said:

Adam: Thank you very much. Wow, it's ice cold. You know this is exactly what I need to drink on my birthday, but what did I do instead? Oh my God! [He continued with hatred ...] *Man, I'm crazy, I've ruined the whole day and my whole life!*

Me: Is it your birthday?

Adam: Yes, it is.

Me: Wow! Happy Birthday to you and to me!

Adam: What do you mean? Is it also your birthday? Are you kidding me?

Me: Yes, it is my birthday! You can see the date on my driver's license! [I showed it to him.]

Adam: Oh yes, happy birthday to you.

Me: Happy birthday to you, too... [I took my candy box out, opened it and held it in front of him...] *Make your night sweet!*

Adam: [With a bitter smile, he picked up a lollipop.] *"Man, I already have ruined it!"*

Me: What did you do?

Adam: Nothing, I just drank a little.

Me: Nothing? So why are you so angry?

Adam: Because I did nothing!

Me: Aha, I got it! How old are you, may I ask?

Adam: 29, and I did nothing in my life. Man, I have done nothing in my life that I can be proud of. I have nothing and I have done nothing…

Me: So?

Adam: …she has finally left me!

Me: Man, at least somebody left you and it is less difficult than if you leave someone! You didn't make anything in your life, but it is less difficult than making something and then losing it or leaving it!

Adam: What do you mean?

Me: Let me tell you my story.

Adam: Sure, go on.

Me: Believe it or not, a few years ago I had to leave my family and country, exactly on my 29th birthday!

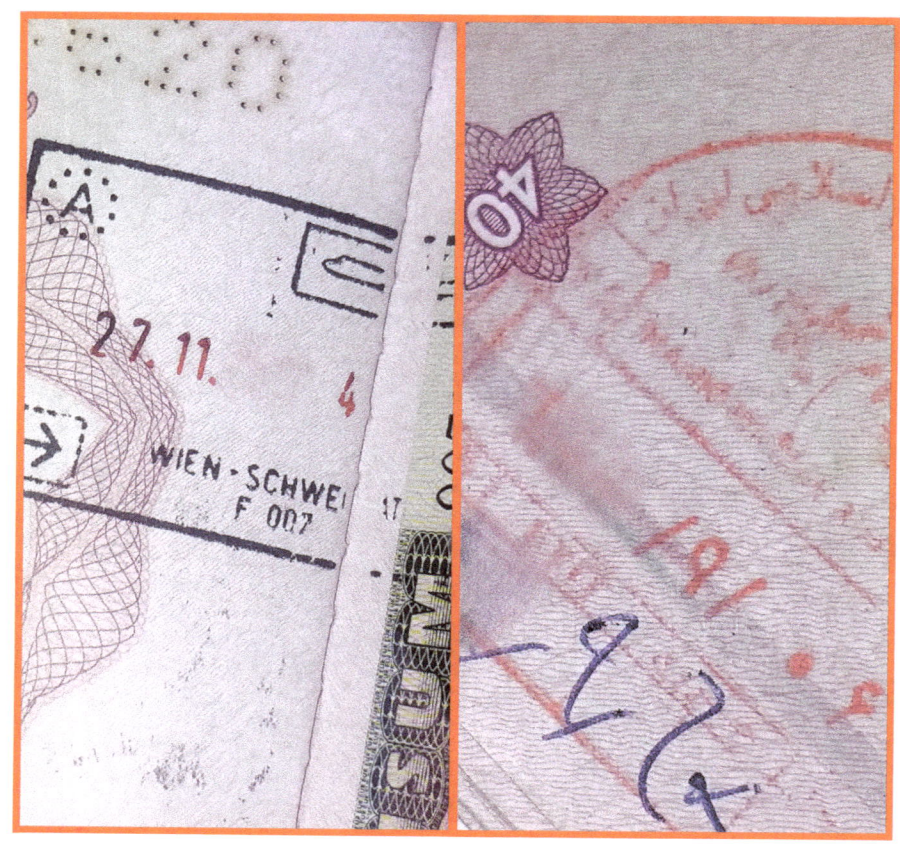

"You don't have any clue about how…

I had my office and my home, and I left them behind. I don't have any of them here!

Adam: So, this is why you work on your birthday! Are you happy?

Me: No, this is not why! I'm making something, I'm doing something! Honestly, I'm not 100% happy, but recently I have learned something that really is helping me feel better…Okay, this is a 25-mile trip, so we have enough time…let me tell you about some true stories which I recently faced and learned from them… [Then I talked about Golshomar, the man with the new legs, Nikoo, and the kids who were fighting cancer. He was completely silent, I explained to him:]

Me: You know that handsome man with those two new legs told me that he is super happy and he feels like he has been reborn. He said that he wants to build a new life. If he can do it, so can we.

Adam: But people have different circumstances.

Me: Exactly! You don't have any clue about how other people got to this starting point that you are now at. Sometimes it is not that easy. Anyway, I learned from Nikoo to stop complaining about my second language and other circumstances! Just do something…

"You don't have any clue about how other people got to this starting point."

Adam: …So you believe that you and your dreamer's hero have an ability to make up something, especially out of the situation that you guys are struggling with?

Me: Honestly, after that trip with my hero, this question and this concern was in my mind for several days. Then I remembered that I had read two research articles from a very famous university. One of them said we have around 34 possible talents, and each person is good at least in five of them. The second article was about if you practice something for 10,000 hours you will become one of the best at it in the world.

Adam: Buddy, I enjoy listening to you, but I don't believe everything that I read!

Me: Okay, let me tell you two things. First, you may be right, but imagine you play a specific video game for 10,000 hours. Do you guess you can be very good at that game after that much practice?

Adam: Yes, of course, but that is crazy if we think in this short life …

Me: …Let me ask you a question, what is the craziest goal for a person who likes writing and who came to the U.S. with almost zero English?

Adam: Write a book in English.

Me: I'm doing it right now! And that book is because of what Golshomar did in her short life. Her life wasn't that long, but she did something in her life…she did something by counting those flowers! …she inspired me and others with that little thing that she could do. You can do something, and it's not too late. Accept your today, just find a goal, try to serve people with that goal, and you will find happiness!

Tomorrow is Thanksgiving Day. Let's be thankful for whatever we have, for starting a new life!

He was crying, but he was happy, and I had explained something that I couldn't completely understand!

Do something and be happy!

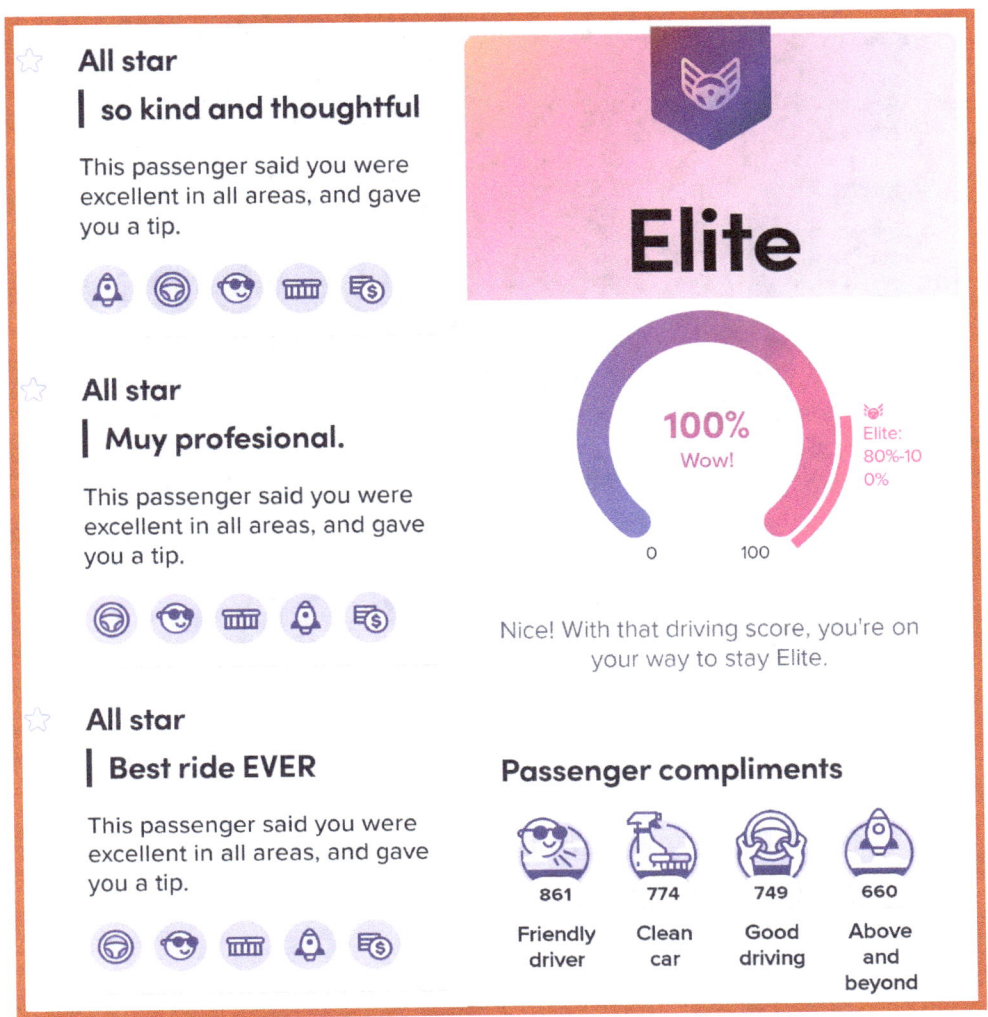

It doesn't matter if we get a compliment once or if we have a month of success. But imagine we have taken 10,000 small steps to success... we can shine even playing a video game!

"It is not necessary to do extraordinary things to get extraordinary results."

"We don't have to be smarter than the rest. We have to be more disciplined than the rest. -Warren Buffett

Here's to 10,000 trips

There's no stopping you, Vasna. Well done on accomplishing this huge milestone.

There is a gap of over two years between when I finished writing this book and when it was ready for publication. During that time, I continued to drive in the Rideshare business to use the trips to market the book, also to improve the statistics. At the time of printing this book, all the statistics, even what I had on the back cover of the book, had grown dramatically better! Something around 14000 trips with still rate 5.

Tip Pages

Happy Birthday!

One of the amenities that I have in my car is a nice box full of candies. One time as a passenger, I got into a car where the driver had left a plate full of candies on the cup holder tray in the back seat.

There were a lot of candies on the plate, and I could also see empty wrapping paper on the plate. That plate didn't look very clean and was covered with stains. This method does not work at all. Candy has no value if it does not make the recipient happy. Keep them out of sight in a clean container and only take them out when the time is right.

I worked on weekends and on Saturday mornings, I often received many ride requests to the airport.

When we arrived at the airport, I would hold the candy box in front of the passengers and say, "I hope you have a sweet and safe flight. Start a sweet day." The look on their faces was spectacular. They felt happy and blessed, and the blessings came back to me as well.

CHAPTER 12

Service Animals

I love animals, but I have a very strange feeling about dogs. I like dogs, but since I was a kid, I've had a fear of getting too close to them. Even though there is no reason for it.

Anyway, one day I accepted a trip request in which at the pick-up point I found out the rider had a huge dog as a service animal. According to the rules, drivers cannot refuse to give rides to riders with service animals, as long as that animal is a real service animal, and it fits in your car. That day I really wanted to give the ride, but I was scared to death of that huge dog.

I always keep two big blankets in my car, one completely white and nice for protecting the passengers' clothes in case the seat is not clean enough. The other blanket is a thick blue one to protect the seat from the animals.

I covered the backseat with the blue blanket. The dog was almost as big as the whole back seat. I let the dog get in the car on his own. I guess he didn't like my hospitality, or he felt that I was afraid. I closed the door and helped the rider to take the front seat, and then I started the trip… Because of the space between my seat and my seat's headrest, and the dog's positioning in the back seat, the dog's tail was right behind my neck. That dog used that space to slap my neck with his tail!

That was not because of wagging the tail at all, I am sure about it! I was so nervous, and I wanted to drive faster to get to the destination as soon as possible. Each time I wanted to increase the speed, the dog would slap me twice. It was just two soft touches on my neck, but it caused me to scream, causing my passenger to laugh after each scream. He kept asking the dog to be nicer to me.

I learned something from that dog: If an animal is that smart to understand the speed limit and care about his owner's safety, there is no reason to fear him or not give your full respect to him.

* * *

Two days later, I accepted a trip request. At the pick-up point, a gentleman and two ladies got into the car's back seat. Then another gentleman carrying a tiny bulldog came in and took the front seat.

The way the man held his dog, the dog's mouth was right next to my right arm. For a few seconds, with great shock and fear, I looked into his face. Jack, the gentleman in the front seat, who was also a funny person, winked at me and said:

Jack: This old man is very nice, and he will sleep on my lap, so don't worry. By the way, he is a service animal! [He winked, I was still hesitant, but I liked his joke, so I responded in a funny tone of voice.]

Me: Oh really? A service animal? What kind of service does he do?

Jack: Joy service!

Me: Joy service? Reallllly… FARRRRT [At that moment, the dog farted. We all exploded in laughter.]

Jack: Yeah …you see!

During the trip, that old dog snored or farted non-stop, and we all laughed so much that tears welled up in our eyes and we had to open the windows!

At the end of the trip Jack told me:

Jack: You did a good service!

Me: No,no, sir. It wasn't me! He did that service! Hahaha!

I asked Jack to let me pet that dog and take a picture of him for my book. It was my very first time to ever pet a mini bulldog. Since then, I am not afraid anymore. That trip and that pet was one of my best experiences in this job. I learned to look without fear and just enjoy!

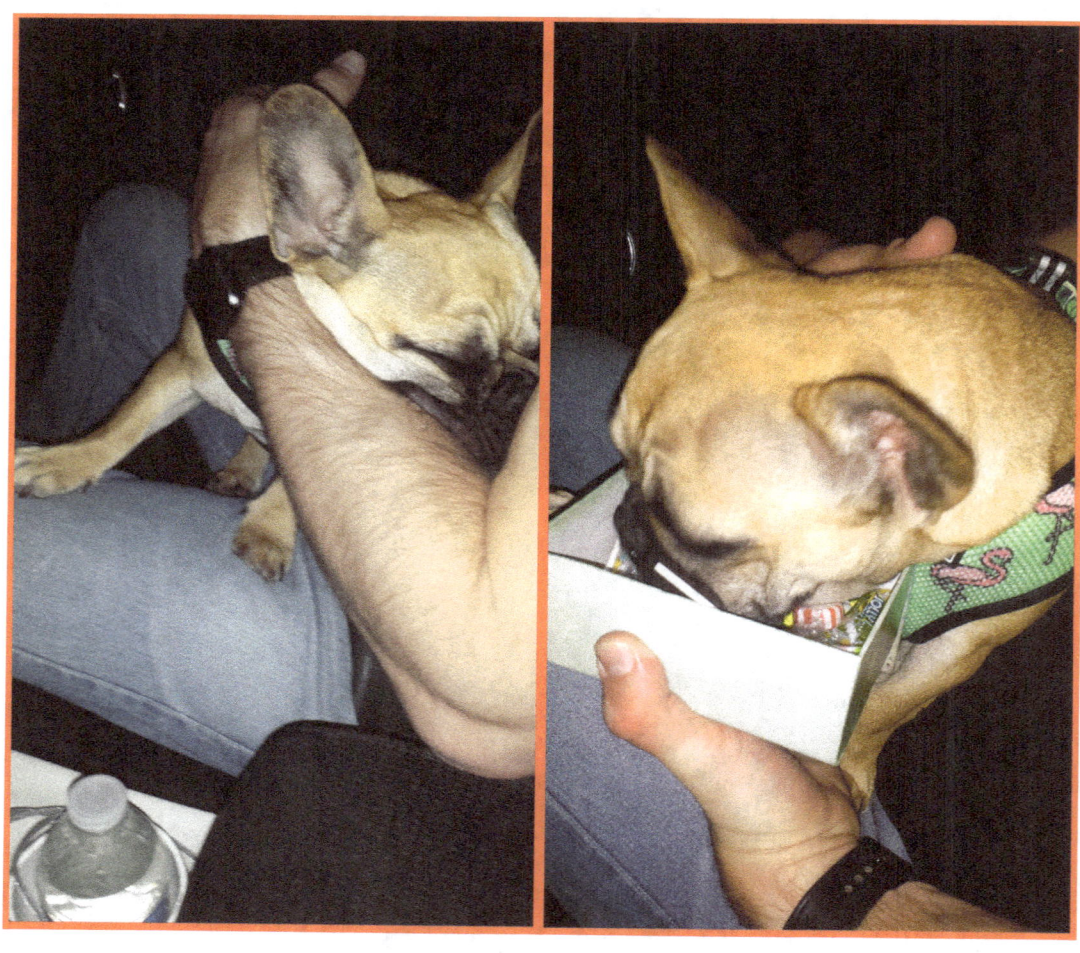

CHAPTER 13

Fair Is Foul?

One Saturday, around noon, as I was coming back to San Diego from a photo shoot, I turned my apps on and set it towards my direction. After a few minutes, I got a shared trip request. As I drove to the pick-up point, an Amtrak station, it started to rain. I was happy because I finished my photo shoot just before the rain could cancel it. When I arrived, I saw there were three riders waiting for me, but the maximum number of passengers allowed in a shared ride is two.

There was a grandmother, a mother, and a kid in a tiny doll stroller, which the kid was too big for.

They didn't seem to be in a good financial situation at all, and I guessed they probably missed the train, and maybe because of the weather they were forced to request a ride.

I pulled over and started talking with the mother.

Me: Excuse me, Ma'am, when you request a shared trip, you can have one more person beside yourself. It means a total of two people per account, but you have two people with yourself and that makes three!

The Mother: No, no, we are just two! She is a little kid. She can sit on my lap.

Me: Ma'am, the app may add another two riders and we don't have seats for them, and your kid cannot sit on your lap. It's not allowed legally. You may lose custody of your child. [There has been some sort of car crash that a divorced parent has lost custody of a child for neglecting to use a child car seat.] *…Also, I may get a traffic violation ticket. This kid should take one full seat and she also should have a car seat. Do you have any…*

The Mother: So, should I cancel the trip? I will get charged a cancellation fee, then my card will be declined for the next ride request because the balance was just enough for getting home on a shared ride.

The Grandmother: My son, please take us home. We are very tired and broke.

It was raining harder, I looked into the eyes of the two women and felt the rain might soon fall from their eyes. I felt that I didn't want them to cancel the trip. I detached the doll stroller and fastened the car's seat belt across it, which made a very safe and secure kid's seat. I put that baby on the seat and when I fastened her seat belt, that innocent kid had tears in her eyes as she looked at my mustache. I don't know why, but she got scared and started to pee on the seat!

Her mother, with a lot of anxiety and great sadness, desperately tried to cover the urine trail with a blanket before I saw it.

I didn't see anything! I didn't want to see!

* * *

At the destination, I helped the grandmother with her stuff and let the mother unlock the seat and help the kid...

I wished for a chance to give that kid a piece of candy from my candy box. Fortunately, I got that opportunity, so I gave her and her grandma some candies, and the child smiled. When she smiled, I was so happy because I myself needed to feel that I am not that scary person who makes a poor family and an innocent kid cry! I don't want to be that person...

* * *

After that ride, I decided to bring forward my car's quarterly interior maintenance, so I went to my favorite car wash for shampooing, vacuuming and steam cleaning the seats.

That night, I had a passenger ask me if I could go to a fast-food drive thru. I accepted and we went to the closest one.

It was another busy night of surge pricing, so I knew I could make more money from my time if I refused to go to drive-thru, but giving a good service to keep my five-star rating was my priority. I mean, he could add a stop to the ride for shopping, but there are always ways the driver can refuse!

He wasn't a nice person; he was extremely impolite. Although I gave him the "Five Star" service that included a bottle of cold water and AUX cable, and I went to a drive-thru for him. When I asked him not to eat inside the car and to wait five minutes to arrive at his destination, he didn't listen. As soon as he got the food, he started eating like a wild animal.

I told him again: *"Please wait! The car was in an expensive car wash today."* His response to my request was an ugly laugh!

After that trip, I started cleaning the car before getting the next passenger. The door's handles and surfaces were greasy, and there were a few ketchup stains on the metal part of seat belt and side window. I also found a tiny sauce stain and plenty of food crumbs on the back seat.

I thought, "*What is fair? What is foul? Are there any consequences for our actions?*"

…That morning I hadn't reported the kid peeing on my car seat to receive a cleaning fee, … this guy's mess was much less than that… *Should I report it to get a cleaning fee? …No! The mess isn't big enough!*

I whispered to myself, "Fair is foul, and foul is fair." But no, it shouldn't be like that…

I was still thinking about those incidents when my phone rang. Because the phone was attached to the dash mount phone holder and I was cleaning the back seat on the back, I couldn't respond. I let it go to voicemail.

Guess what? The voicemail was from that ugly, foul passenger. He called me through the app's customer service line, and he called because he had dropped his wallet under the seat while he was eating wildly!

I found the wallet. Then a lady who was the driver support representative called me and asked about the wallet. I told her that I had found it. I let her know the entire problem that I had with that passenger and that I didn't want to go and return the wallet to him directly because I didn't have a good feeling about him.

Honestly, I felt that I don't want to spend more time with that guy, and he doesn't deserve my favor!

The representative told me, "*Please keep the wallet in a safe place. Monday is a holiday, so please bring it to the Greenlight office on Tuesday. Also, we don't charge the riders for that size of mess, but we charged him $80 because we should support fair and in this case, he did…*"

I don't remember what she said after that, except for one word. She said "fair." I was shocked!

CHAPTER 14

So Close, So Far

On Friday nights, downtown San Diego is really fun and full of people who enjoy themselves. One Friday night, I got a rider from downtown who wanted to go somewhere about 40 miles to the north. Then I got another ride another 10 miles farther north. Most drivers like to go back to downtown because there are more surges, more rides and more fun!

I remember as my third ride, I picked up a guy from a local pub, his account name was "Will." He looked a little sad. I offered him a bottle of cold water and he started to talk to me.

Will: Did you have a good night?

Me: Yes, a very good one. How about you?

Will: Huh, it was okay! Do you work in this area?

Me: Yes and no! Less than an hour ago, I was in downtown San Diego.

Will: Wow, so far away!

Me: Hmm, not really, less than an hour.

I looked at his face for a moment. He was staring forward with glassy eyes and was deep in thought.

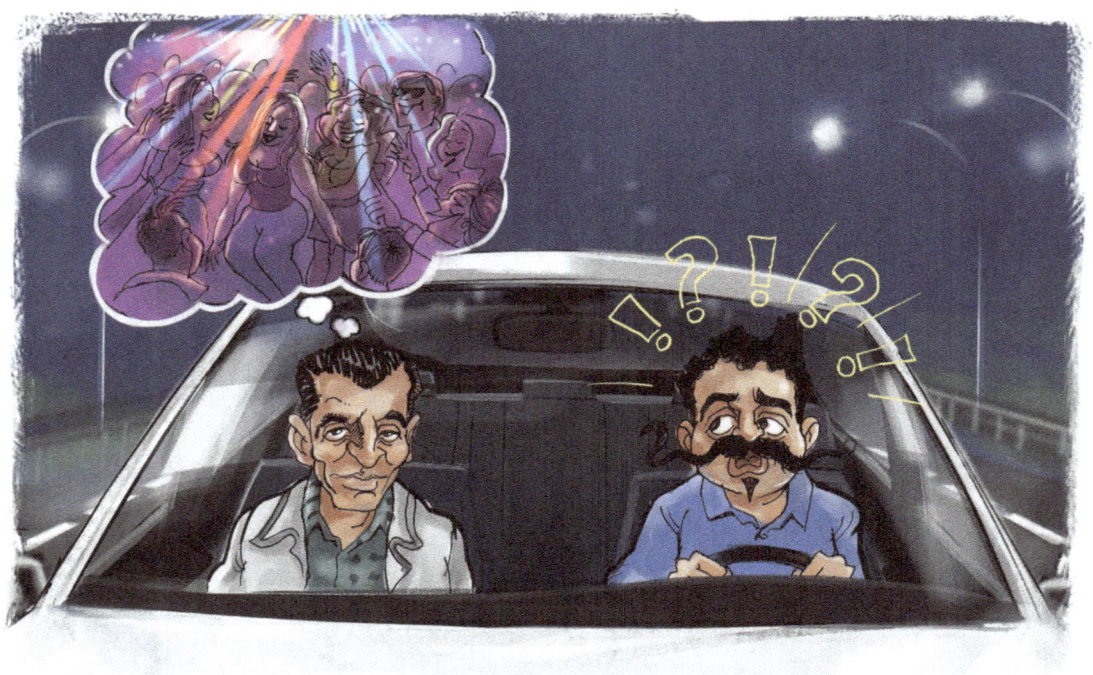

Will: How crowded was it there?

Me: Hmm, a little more than every Friday because there was a game in the Petco Park Stadium…they [the Padres] *won and the people were so happy.*

Will: Oh, I wish I could be there tonight and enjoy myself. Aah, I wish I could…You know, I really enjoy being there, but it's been almost ten years since the last time that I was there. Now, it is like an unattainable dream for me.

Me: Whaaat? Dream!? Why dream? Let's go! I'm going there right now, just change the drop-off point and we can go there together!

Will: Oh no, maybe another time. One day I will…

Me: Is it too expensive for you to pay for the ride and come to downtown with me right now?

Will: Hmmmm, I can afford it.

Me: So why don't we go…?

Will: Ahhh no, I have to work tomorrow evening.

Me: Evening!?

Will: 5 p.m.

Me: No…what I mean was … anyway… I have a question, please …

Will: Go on.

Me: You came to this pub today. Why didn't you go to downtown instead?

Will: Too far…

Me: Sir, it is only about fifty miles and less than an hour from your home, you came to the west to that pub, you could go to the south to downtown!

Will: I know…, it's easy to say, but life forces us to follow whatever is necessary for us.

Me: Sir, let me tell you something, please. I was in three consecutive trip promotions, so I needed to give three rides in a row to receive that bonus. This ride is the third one, and by finishing this ride, I will receive that bonus. I'd like to go back to downtown so I'll have to head over there, but this app is exactly like life: If I don't take any action, it will give me another trip and another, and send me to somewhere else so I don't get to downtown at the right time that I want…

Will: But you followed the life's rules for getting that bonus, so this is why you are here. Correct?

Me: Hmmmm. Yes, you are right, sometimes I follow the app and sometimes I set it toward my desired direction because I know I want to get there, and the most important thing is I wouldn't postpone it until it becomes too late. Please don't postpone what you want, just do it, please.

Will: I will, I will!

* * *

I had read a quote from the Dalai Lama that said: *"I believe that the very purpose of life is to be happy… I have found out that the more we care for the happiness of others, the greater is our own sense of well-being."*

The next day, I couldn't stop thinking about Will. I thought that sometimes our dreams are not that far from us, but we are not brave enough to take small steps. We just postpone our dreams to a "tomorrow" that never comes. Also, we don't help each other make a dream come true, and that is sad, really sad!

I thought happiness in life could be just these little joys, this little help that we give and receive, and these adventures that we can talk about with our kids years later.

Anyway, that night around 11 p.m., my last passenger was a nursing supervisor from an ER. Her name was Katie, and when I arrived at the pick-up point, Katie called me and asked if I could wait five more minutes for her because something happened, and she needed to double-check it. I told her that I would wait, so I parked somewhere and turned my hazard lights on and started to look at the drawing of my cartoon face on my phone. It was for the cover of this book.

I looked at all the details and I laughed at it. Then all of a sudden, Katie opened the door and saw me laughing. She got into the back seat of the car and told me:

Katie: Thank you for waiting for me.

Me: Hi. You are welcome. What's the account name?

Katie: I could see you from the window when we were talking on the phone, I'm Katie.

Me: Perfect. Good to go?

Katie: Yes, we are good to go. Just please tell me, what was so funny on your phone? You were looking at something and laughing when I arrived. Maybe it would help me laugh because I really need to feel good right now.

[I showed her that cartoon. She laughed.]

Katie: Wow that's your cartoon. It looks like your profile photo.

Me: Exactly. I made it for the cover of my book.

Katie: Really? Do you have a book?

Me: I'm writing it now.

Katie: Are you a writer?

Me: Yes and no. This is my first book in English, but I used to write scripts for shows and screenplays for movies in my language.

Katie: Cool! I love literature and I am very talented. I wanted to become a writer, but I decided to go to nursing school because of life, but one day when I retire, I will definitely start writing…even thinking about that dream makes me feel great.

Me: You said that you need a good feeling, and writing makes you feel great, so why don't you start writing now? Why do you want to postpone it until your retirement? You need to be happy right now.

Katie: Because I don't know how to do it. I mean, first I want to learn to write better.

Me: There are many good online classes and video tutorials. Recently, I saw very good videos from James Patterson. He is really a master. Those videos would totally take less than three hours. Watch them, then start.

Katie: Do you see why I cannot start now? I have to go and buy the videos first, watch them, then start to write. Anyway, I will retire next fall and I can start it at that time.

Me: But you need a good feeling now, so let me teach you a way that you can at least write something to enjoy…

Katie: …Sure.

Me: Every day, at the end of the day, for a few minutes, write down the most interesting thing that happened to you. Do it like a movie scene.

Katie: I don't know how to write a movie scene.

Me: Okay, imagine this is a scene that happened inside of an Uber. From the moment that you opened the door of my car to the moment that you closed the door at the destination, just write down everything you saw and heard in detail. No complicated introductions, openings, endings, or even characterization are required. Without any great sentences, just write whatever you saw and write it in a way that if somebody reads it, that person can imagine that scene. That's all. Just every time that you need a good feeling, just write a scene, and next fall you'll have a book with too many short stories, and all of them have the same character: you!

When we reached the destination, her eyes were shining from the good feeling that she needed. She gave me a fifty-dollar bill as a tip and told me: *"Show this really funny cartoon to all your passengers. You will make a lot of money from the people who enjoy it, and who enjoy talking with you."*

Oh, what a great idea! Her words and of course that fifty-dollar bill sparked something in my mind! I set that cartoon as my cell phone's home screen…believe me I got over a thousand dollars extra in tips from the people who saw it and enjoyed finding out what it is for! Over 2,000 people left my car telling me it was the best ride ever, and they are looking to buying my book!

I learned that from Katie!

Thank you, Katie.

Zoroaster, the ancient Persian prophet who was also a scholar and great thinker said, *"Happiness comes to them who bring happiness to others."*

CHAPTER 15

Music Is A Language

I love many kinds of music, but at the same time, I am a little picky and strict about what music I listen to. The first year that I came to the U.S., I went to a class about music and the production process. In that class, just like in American society, there were people of many different cultures, races, and backgrounds therefore they liked a wide range of music.

We, the students, were required to introduce our favorite music and present a project that detailed the steps we would take to produce that music, a music that makes every person in the audience come together in a perfect union! A music that we feel is close to who we are and what we really like. It was a difficult project and I remember that year I was also in a photography class that had a lot of difficult projects. I was very frustrated, especially because for a while I was feeling that the professor of the photography class treated me differently and his behavior was due to hatred and racism. One day he told me, *"You are Iranian, but like that Italian guy, Houdini, you can do magic and surprise people without any equipment and with your bare hands!"* I thought why did he mention the name of my country? Why did he say such a thing? If I were him, I would never mention such categories! By the way, Houdini was Hungarian! He was a Hungarian-American escape artist and a magician who is noted for his escape acts! After the class I was upset and on my way to the music class, I thought if I were him, I would never label people with racist labels. Oh, no, no...never!!

Anyway, when I got to the class, Taylor, the music class teacher was there. He was white-skinned, a bit strict but polite and nice guy, probably of Euro-American racial background! The rest of the students had not yet arrived, I had a question, and it was a good time to ask. First, he paid me a compliment.

Taylor: I really enjoyed the amazing music that you introduced. Again, what was the name of that instrument?

*Me: Persian **santur*** and the other one was **tombak***.*

Taylor: Yeah, I know tombak. Great. Bring more music videos like these.

Me: Actually, sir, let me ask you a question. This bothers me most of the time in class and makes my mind busy.

---

* Tombak or Tonbak is a Persian music instrument, for more information and see related video, please scan the QR codes at the end of this chapter...

Taylor: Sure, go on…

Me: … Sir, I wonder why you let some of the students play those annoying ear-bothering noises as music? [I was referring to the music that some students played in class, and I really didn't like it, I felt they were annoying and ear-splitting]

Taylor: Do you know what makes America great? Collecting a wide variety of talents, brains and brawn from different races, cultures, and backgrounds, respecting them, and using them to build this great country. You should respect people's favorite music. Everyone's favorite music is a key to their soul. It is the best tool to communicate, get close to, and make peace with people when no common language is present. We need to respect people's favorite music as it is their father's, their mother's, and their race's! We cannot talk like we are better than the others, or our favorite thing is more important…We shouldn't be racist. Music is for peace.

Remember, we respect their souls when it is touched by that music. It is a way that we as artists can grow!

That question was one of the silliest questions I had ever asked, and his answer was humbling. After what he said, I forgot to ask my main question! I left but learned a great lesson.

Another shameful thing that I realized that day was when I reviewed everything that had gone through my mind after the photography class. I got an A from the professor whom I thought was racist and would never give me an A! I reviewed that in my mind and felt even more embarrassed because I got that A when I really didn't think that I deserved it.

I realized that, regardless of color and race, each of us can unknowingly have racist behaviors but at the same time accuse other people of it, just because, we cannot see the plank when it is in our own eyes*!

* * *

Years after that lesson, one morning around 3:45 a.m. I picked up four happy passengers from what looked like an Airbnb place. Their average ages were around 20 and they were going to the border station.

When they got into the car, one of those guys asked me if I have an AUX cable. I thought to myself, *"Oh God. it is 3:45 a.m.!"*

I didn't want to, but I passed the AUX to him. He played music and very politely asked me if he could make it louder. I told him that since this is a residential area, we'll need to first enter the highway. Then, he could turn up the music as much as he wanted.

A minute later, we entered the highway, and he asked me if he could turn the volume up, and I said yes as promised. He put it almost to the maximum! Unfortunately, I needed to keep my word!

---

* *Book of Matthew 7:3*

That early morning, they were absolutely enjoying their time in my car. Full of energy, they were singing with the music as loud as they could!

What was the lyric? It was something like: If you want money, first you need a few hookers with Cocaine! They really enjoyed it and sang together with a great passion.

I found it super annoying, but I had to keep my word. I reminded myself that I have to respect their favorite music. Those young people were very polite and perfectly normal, and they were just enjoying the music, so I said to myself, *"I'm going to focus on my driving and let them enjoy their trip as much as they can."*

It was very strange but after a few minutes, I also was enjoying the very positive feeling and the energy that was in my car!

I couldn't believe that one day I would enjoy listening to something like that, not because it's good or bad but because it was not my taste. I enjoyed it. I felt at peace. I got a five-star rating, plus an unbelievable tip, which was very unusual from passengers in that age group.

* * *

On long trips, the "absolute silence" inside the car may bother some passengers, but sometimes it is very difficult to find a conversation topic. When the passenger looks more formal, classy, and rich, starting a conversation that is pleasant for everyone becomes even harder. On a short trip, finding something to talk about with that particular group of people is almost impossible!

I remember, the great Italian singer Andrea Bocelli was coming to San Diego; and almost two months later, André Rieu, the great Dutch composer and violinist, was coming.

I really wished I could get tickets for both events, but first, I needed to work on my goals and then financially, getting tickets to both events were a bit of a splurge for me. So, by coin flip I decided to work as a driver on the night of Bocelli's concert and instead go to Rieu's concert.

The night of the Bocelli concert, I was sad because I missed that concert. I picked up a well-dressed couple from the concert hall, the trip was only two miles to a nearby hotel, where they had a room. I was very curious to know how the concert was. Although the couple seemed reluctant to talk, I took the risk of making them angry [not every rider wants to talk] to ask about the concert.

"How was Bocelli?" I asked.

The lady eagerly said, *"It was wonderful and dreamy,"* then the gentleman asked me, *"Do you know him?"* I told them about the coin flip between Bocelli and Rieu's concert and I told them I'm a fan of both great artists.

I told them how I am sad that I couldn't go to the first concert, but on the other hand, I'm seeing Rieu and would be glad if he plays "And the Waltz Goes On" by Anthony Hopkins.

They were shocked because they didn't know about that specific musical piece. When we arrived at the hotel, they didn't want to leave my car and asked questions about that piece, so I searched for it on Google, and they wanted to keep watching the video inside the car! They finally left!

That night, they tipped me about six times the fare. The funny thing was when they got out of the car, they thanked me like I had performed for them!

Kahlil Gibran, a Lebanese-American writer who is one of my favorite thinkers says: "Music is the language of the spirit. It opens the secret of life bringing peace, abolishing strife."

* * *

After those two stories, for a while I was thinking about how I could use music to increase the quality of my service? I thought of doing an experiment and examining the effects of soft background music on passengers' reactions. It was close to Christmas. In the very first experiment, I found a very cool radio station and played it for the first passenger.

What was his reaction? He said, *"Oh my God! No! No! No! …No more 'Jingle Bells.' Noooooo! I am listening to this song eight hours in a row at the bookstore where I'm working. Pull over, I will walk!"*

The experiment failed hilariously!

For more information about those instruments and see related video, please scan the QR codes.

CHAPTER 16

Water is blessed

One of the reasons I really like this job is because it provided me the opportunity to conduct fun experiments in the socioeconomic fields. Although none of those experiences can be scientifically presented and explored, I really enjoyed doing them. I did eleven different experiments, but there's one I really want to share. I called it "Water experiment" and I did it when I was giving bottles of cold water to riders. That experiment was fun to do, and the reason I became interested in doing that experiment was because of a funny story that happened in my car!

Before telling the story let me mention something. When I started this job from the first week [right after the story of those water bottles that happened on my first day and I've already told it], I decided to offer a cold bottle of water the same way — with great respect — to every rider, no matter if the type of trip was shared, pool, X or Express, and no matter if the passenger looked rich or poor. I did it for every rider over more than 7,000 trips.

There is a belief in my culture that says whoever bakes bread for the hungry people and whoever gives water to thirsty people will get blessed.

When I decided to give water to each and every passenger, I was one hundred percent sure that I would benefit from that. I gave it to people absolutely free and without any expectation, though. It gave me a very good feeling. Some passengers enjoyed drinking it for free and some other added tips to the trips, but during the whole time that I gave water to the passengers, I didn't lose even a cent, especially since the IRS lets a driver deduct the costs of all the amenities from his taxes.

Every single week, I made a minimum of 500% of the amount that I spent on the water, and the unparalleled number of five-star ratings I got was another benefit of this decision.

Anyway, one night a funny story sparked the idea of doing the "Water experiment" in my mind, especially since I had already discussed something about marketing and water with my friend Jahan in his frozen yogurt store!

That night, I got a trip request in front of a very expensive and private club/restaurant. A very well-dressed couple waited for me, and the man wore big dark sunglasses, which was a little weird to me since it was 11 p.m.

The account name was "Hanks," and once he confirmed that he was Hanks, I started the trip. But before I could offer the water to them, the couple started talking to each other. I didn't want to interrupt them because it's not polite. So, I was silent, and waited for a good moment to offer them the bottles of water. That lady, who was probably Hanks' wife, spoke to him.

Hanks' wife: I didn't like the wine that much.

Hanks: Yeah, but it was a $200 bottle of wine.

Hanks' wife: Really?

Hanks: Yeah, look at the receipt…I knew something was wrong with it, but one of the waiters recognized who I was and asked to take a selfie with me, so I forgot to double check the receipt over there.

Hanks' wife: What's wrong with it?

Hanks: We were six people, so I wanted to add at least an 20% tip. The bill was $1,232, so I needed to give something around $247, but I only gave $200.

She said, *"Oh My God"* and I said, *"Ooooh My Goood!"* in my mind because it shocked me and also made me very curious. I didn't want to purposely listen to their conversation, but I couldn't help…I overhear them when I was just seeking a good time to offer them the water.

From what I heard, I guessed Hanks might be famous. A question flashed in my mind: Is he Tom Hanks? Tom Hanks is one of my most favorite actors ever and meeting him would be a dream come true for me. It was dark and that man didn't look like Tom Hanks, but I needed to make sure because if he was in my car, I couldn't lose that opportunity. I wanted to at least take a selfie with him, maybe for my book! I thought I needed to see his face better.

Me: Sir, I can turn the cabin light on so you can see the receipt better.

Hanks: Sure, please do it. Thank you.

I turned the light on, and he wasn't Tom Hanks. I thought, *"Should I offer them water when they didn't even like a $200 bottle of wine?"* Then I said to myself, *"I will do it because of my promise and my belief, but they probably don't want it, and even they may not like hearing such an offer."*

I offered the water, and that lady immediately accepted it!

She really enjoyed drinking the water and said that bottle of water was the best thing she had for the entire night. While she was drinking, Hanks called that restaurant and talked with the manager.

Every minute, I got more surprised. He called and apologized for not paying enough tips because of a mistake. He asked the manager to charge him $50 more on his credit card and add it to the tip. When he took care of the receipt, he looked at his wife with a big smile...

Hanks: Mahna Mahna! Hahahaha. That funny music was another reason that I messed up with my math.

Hanks' wife: Hahaha, that was very interesting music. Mike played it from his cellphone, hahaha. What was that?

Hanks: I don't know. It was something like "Mahna Mahna!" Do do dodo do…

Hanks' wife: Yes! Hahahaha! I even forgot to thank them. That music brought tears to my eyes! Hahahaha!

I knew exactly what music they were talking about. That song was from the very first episode of "The Muppet Show." Years ago, when my brother and his wife were making a puppet show in my country, we analyzed that lovely and very popular show to get some ideas for our own show. When the couple talked about that song, I had the video of that song in my other phone, and I gave it to them to watch.

They played that music more than three times and laughed the whole trip. At the drop-off point, Hanks said, *"What good service. Thank you so much,"* and they left.

During the trip, I did math in my mind, thinking to myself that if Hanks gives me just a $3 tip, I will have reached my Saturday goal of $250 and I can go home. I thought that since this guy gave a $250 tip that easily, probably he will give me a good tip, especially since I played that song for them as well. It was the first and the only time that I expected a tip, and only because I wanted to go home after that trip.

I said to myself, *"I'm done with my night, let's go home."* Guess how much he tipped me? Zero! He played the song, and he laughed a lot and probably forgot it. Mahna Mahna, Hahaha!!

Experiment

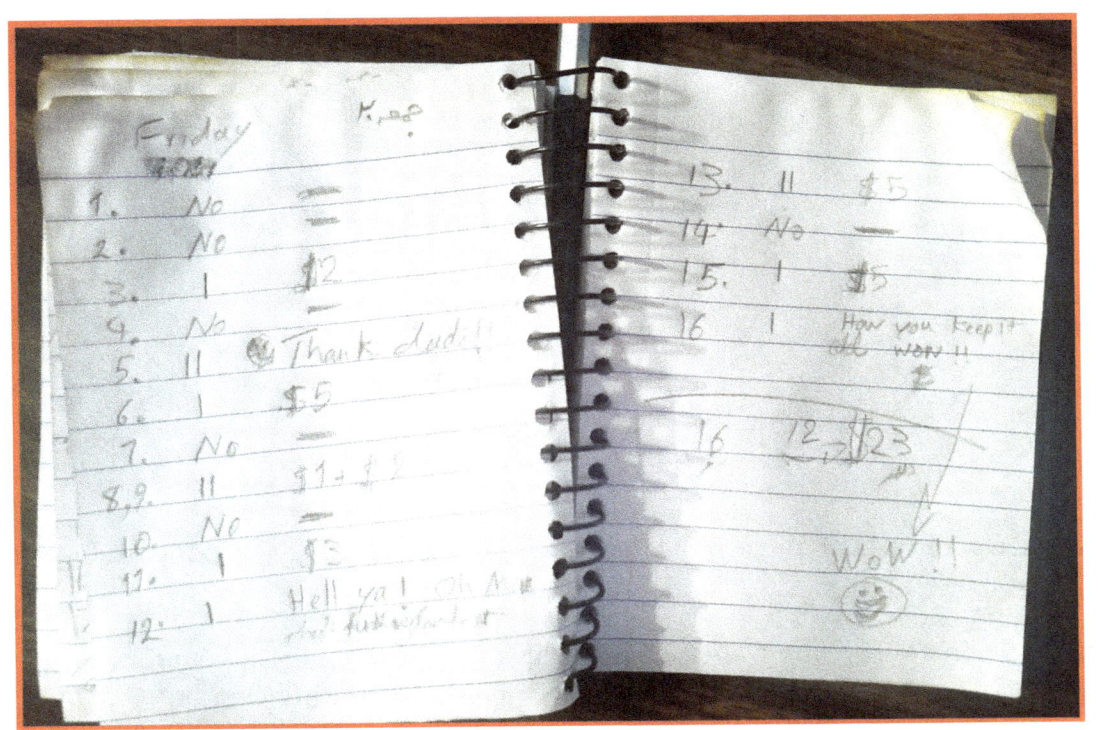

Passenger / Trip	Water Bottle	Reacation / Outcome
1.	NO	---
2.	NO	---
3.	🍶	$ 2
4.	NO	---
5.	🍶🍶	Thanks dude !
6.	🍶	$ 5
7.	NO	---
8.	🍶	$ 1
9.	🍶	$ 2
10.	NO	---
11.	🍶	$ 3
12.	🍶	Hell ya, Oh man that's perfect !!
13.	🍶🍶	$ 5
14.	NO	---
15.	🍶	$ 5
16.	🍶	WoW !! How do you keep it so cold ?!
Total:16	12x 🍶	$ 23 + Good feeling + LOL

A night: Total trips = 16, Bottles = 12, Cost = $ 1.81, Tip = $23
A week: Total trips = 69, Bottles = 49, Cost = $ 7.43, Tip = $98

CHAPTER 17

Wash it All!

People who are very strict about keeping their cars clean probably have experienced Murphy's Law when it comes to car washes!

For those who don't know who Murphy and his law are, Edward Aloysius Murphy Jr. (January 11, 1918 – July 17, 1990) was an American aerospace engineer who worked on safety-critical systems. When an attempt to use a new measurement device that Murphy developed failed, Murphy blamed his assistant, saying, *"If that guy has any way of making a mistake, he will."* This eventually evolved into "If anything can go wrong, it will" or "Anything that can go wrong will go wrong."

Of course, I guess this is the negative form of what is known as the law of attraction, which states positive or negative thoughts bring positive or negative experiences into a person's life. But no matter, I only want to tell a funny story about it and the solution that I found to stay away from the bad impact of those crazy experiences.

You probably have heard many people say that every time they go to the car wash, it starts raining. For a long time, I really believed it until...

Before starting the story, I need to mention that I have a bit of an obsessive-compulsive personality, so as a driver with OCD*, I wanted to keep my five-star rating and I was super-sensitive about my car's interior and exterior cleanliness. Every day, I cleaned my car thoroughly, and I frequently went to the car wash as well, but it seemed like every single time, something immediately happened to my car right after carwash.

When I say immediately, I mean within five minutes!

---

*   *OCD: Obsessive-Compulsive Disorder*

Oh dear !? Dear seagull, believe me I'm worried about your health! This is not normal at all! You have diarrhea! Please go see your primary health provider!!!

This crazy thinking got to the point that whenever I wanted to go to the car wash, I first checked the weather forecast; and while at the car wash, before my car left the washing area, I always looked everywhere to make sure no birds awaited me!

He is coming, he is comiiiing... Do it! Dooo it! Ready ... aim ...fire!

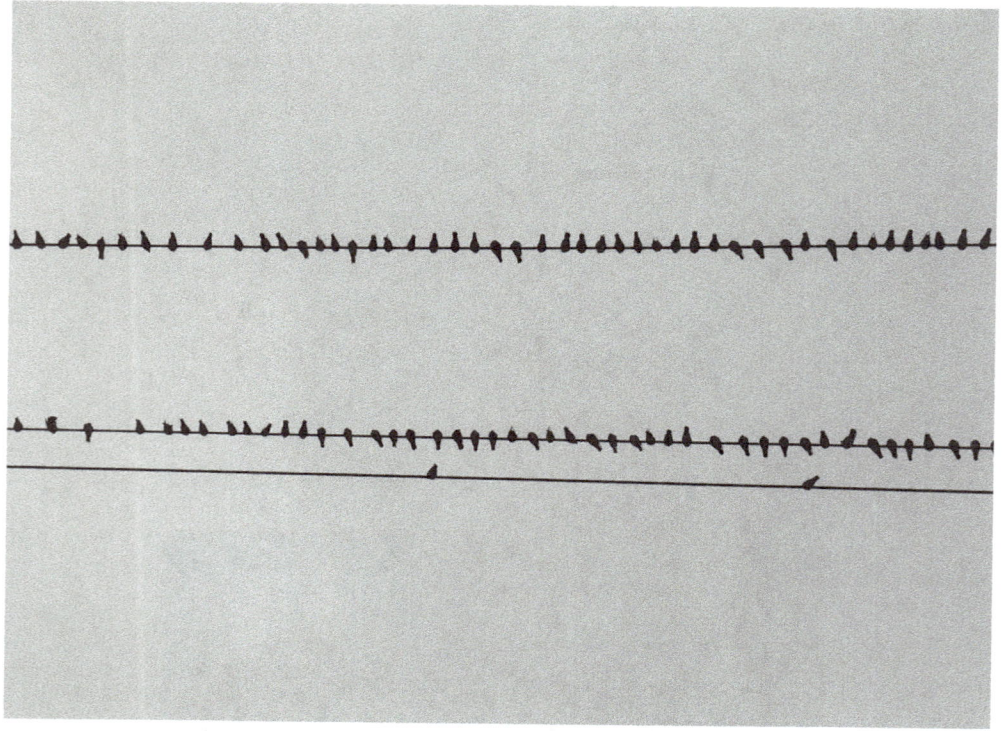

I had that negative feeling about "after carwash" and unfortunately it was not just about my car's exterior! Every time that I shampooed and polished the interior, I got nervous something was going to happen and it did most of the times. (see the story in "Fair is Foul?").

I remember besides those daily cleanings and weekly going to carwash every three months I used to pay for an expensive service to get my car detailed.

* * *

One-day right after one of those expensive detailing services, I received a trip request. The passenger was a former rideshare driver and he grumbled about how his app got permanently deactivated because his star rating for two weeks in a row had been lower than the required rate to work. His name was Eihab, and he was angry!

I gave him all the amenities and the best service that I could, but he wasn't happy at all with the way I treated him. I guess my good service angered him more! He started twisting one of my phone chargers around his finger and said:

Eihab: Your car shouldn't be this clean! Why do you keep these phone chargers here, plugged, and ready to use?

Me: The price of this charger is 99 cents. I bought it from one of those dollar stores. You cannot imagine how many times passengers thank and tip me just because of that charger! For a while, I was taking notes and counting the times, it went even over $200. Then I gave up and stopped taking notes, but people still use it and appreciate this idea. Anyway, may I ask what caused your rate to go down?

Eihab: Crazy people had reported my car and said it didn't smell good. B.S.! I cannot control the smell of the car and riders, can you?

Me: First of all, my car doesn't smell bad because it gets cleaned every day. Let me tell you something: I used to do cologne photography, so I know many good, light and cool smelling cologne, and I use some of those in my car, and surely, I have 100% control of it.

Eihab: B.S.! I cannot spend money on cologne for a car that people may throw up in!

Me: Nobody threw up in my car because I have at least four thick plastic bags ready in front of each seat. Also, why can't you pay for it? Buddy, this is business. Look, I have a bottle of cologne here on my console which I bought for $73, and I use it just for business. I keep it in my car, and it is enough for almost four months. In less than two weeks from the time that I bought it, the cologne has been paid off with the tips that mostly ladies added to the trips. They were giving tips right after mentioning the great smell of my car.

Eihab: That's really nonsense! You also give them water and chargers and good services. You cannot say the tips were just because of the cologne.

Me: I just counted the people who mentioned the great smells and didn't get the water, but you are right, this statistic is not that reliable. The point is, in those two weeks, I spent $148 for all amenities (including the price of the cologne and the costs of water and car wash) and I made a total of $289 in tips, both cash and on the app. The cost of amenities for a week is not always that much. It varies between $16 to $80, but even with the maximum of costs, those tips will pay for everything.

Eihab: Don't say it like that. After deducting the costs, you only made $10 in tips each day, I can make it by handling a passenger's heavy luggage in front of the airport.

Me: You miscalculated because I don't work in this job every day of the week! It was about $50 each day... and yes, you might be able to make it if you could keep the job, but you don't have it anymore! Sir, you're not listening to me, instead of fighting with me to pull me down, take my hand to come up...Do you know what "Crab mentality" is?*

Eihab: Huuuuh I don't know, and I don't want to know, pull over! I don't want to listen to your bullshit anymore!

He slammed the door and left. Later, I found out that he gave me a bad rating. The funniest thing was that he had left nasty, sticky dirt on the door and reported my car as a dirty, bad smelling car!

I learned it's not a good idea to argue with the riders at all!

---

* *Crab mentality also known as crab theory or the crab-bucket effect, is a way of thinking best described by the phrase "if I can't have it, neither can you". The metaphor is derived from a pattern of behavior noted in crabs when they are trapped in a bucket. While any one crab could easily escape, its efforts will be undermined by others, ensuring the group's collective demise.*

> # Recent feedback
>
> ## Vehicle cleanliness
>
> 1 report
>
> With multiple riders coming and going through your vehicle every day, it can be hard to make sure your vehicle is always clean. Highly rated drivers tell us they check their vehicle for trash after they drop off their riders.
>
>

Multiple riders?! That ride was my first trip right after the car wash!

I remember that day was my day off and it was close to Christmas. I don't usually drive in daylight, but I picked up Eihab on my way home after coming back from one of those expensive carwashes. He was my first rider right after the carwash. Aside from the false feedback he had posted, he also left nasty dirt in my car.

During the day I thought a lot about him, and I was feeling sad and even angry, but finally I said to myself, *"If somebody doesn't deserve to be carried in my car, why should I carry him in my mind!"* I forgot about him, but I didn't forget about Murphy's Law. I still thought something else may happen to the interior of my car after this car wash.

* * *

At night when I felt better, I went to work. I got a shared request from three different accounts, a middle-aged couple, a young girl, and a man. The man was going home from work, but the other three were going home from their companies' Christmas parties. They were super drunk from drinking too much at the "open bars", so I gave them plastic bags and all of them started to throw up. I couldn't believe that one day I would need to use three out of four bags I had in my console, all at the same time!

I immediately pulled over, asked the young girl to move to the back seat, moved the man who wasn't drunk to the front seat, offered him mint gum, turned the AC to the maximum cold and rolled down the windows a little.

The first destination was the man who felt fine. He smiled and thanked me for that gum!

I had a strange feeling, I felt that was the worst trip that I had ever had, but nothing happened to the cleanliness of my car. I did my best, and I handled it!

Also, I learned how to handle this situation for the future!

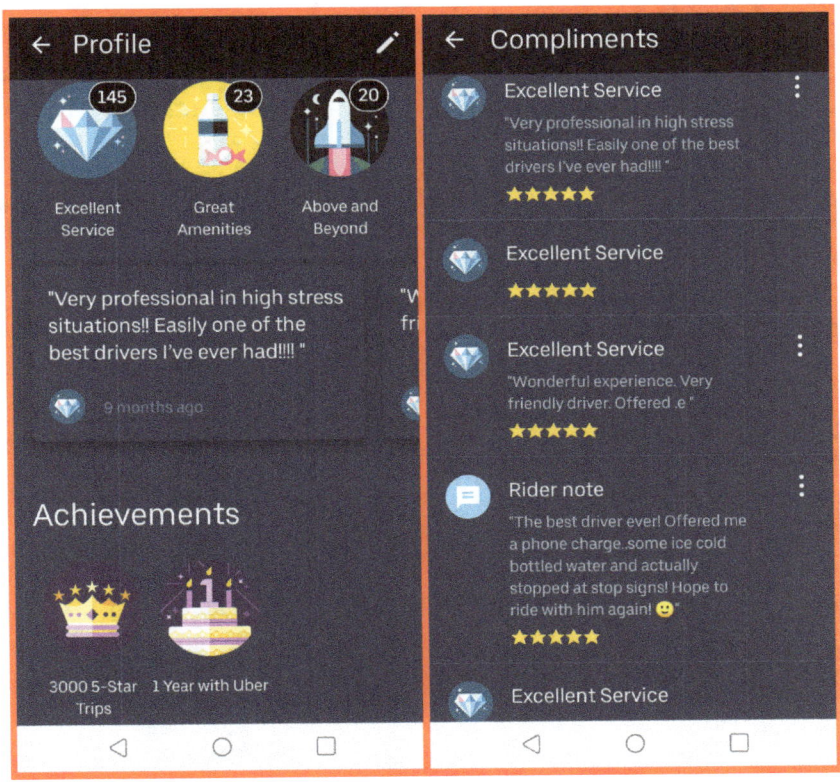

After that trip, I signed a very affordable monthly contract for unlimited use of the car wash, which greatly reduced my expenses and made my car even cleaner. Then I thought to myself that I could go to the car wash every day and I'm sure it won't rain every day! I have no reason to be sensitive about it because I am prepared.

Being prepared and not being overly sensitive was the secret that removed the stress and when it happened, suddenly, Murphy's Law lost its power in my mind! I had washed it all away!

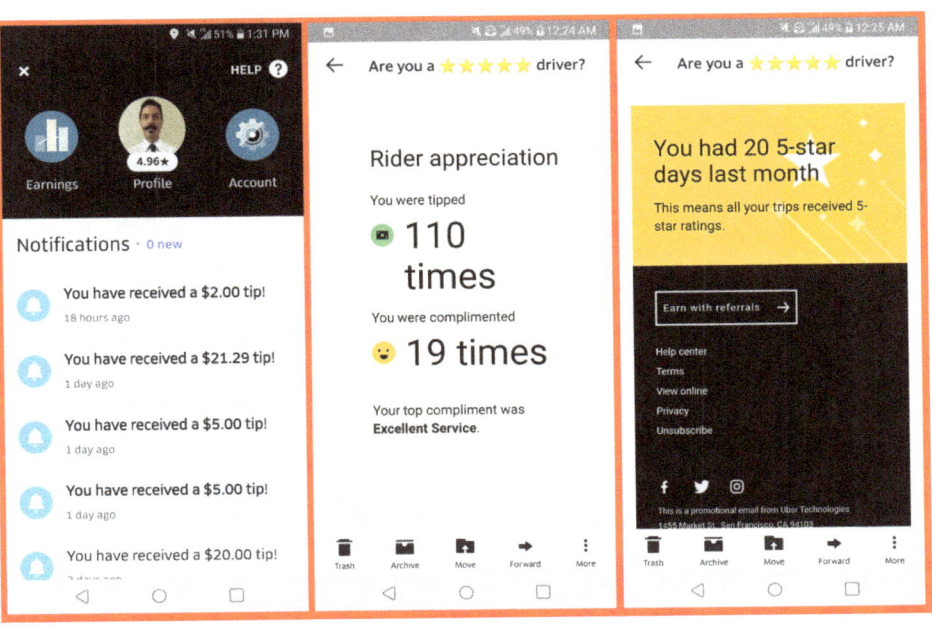

≡ **Your feedback**

Excellent

Well done! Your rating (5.0) and account status are in great shape.

★ 5.0

Last 100 rides

Compliments All time

298 | **278** | **273** | **161**

Friendly driver | Clean car | Good driving | Above and beyond

Feedback Earlier

⭐ **All star**

This passenger said you were excellent in all areas.

⭐ **Ride hero**

| **He's such a good man. He ma**

This passenger complimented you: friendly driver, good driving.

⭐ **Ride hero**

This passenger gave you a tip, and complimented you: clean car, good driving.

⭐ **All star**

This passenger said you were excellent in all areas, and gave you a tip.

Tip Pages

I paid a small fee to buy all the usual cell phone chargers such as iPhone, Android and Type C. I connected them in front of the passenger seat and made them available and ready to use. At the beginning of the trip as part of my greeting, I let the passengers know that they were welcome to use them. You cannot believe how grateful some passengers were.

Once at the drop-off point in front of the airport, I gifted one of my extra chargers to a passenger who forgot his charger at home and was very upset and said his day was ruined. I said, "Dude, please take mine. You can have it for free. Don't ruin your day." Then I also gave him a lollipop! He laughed loudly. I gave him that charger to prevent him from ruining his day and vacation. I just wanted to help him. Later, I found out that he added a $20 tip to the ride. That money was enough to buy several new chargers and replace all worn out one!

I also had an AUX cable for playing music through the car stereo. Although it was connected and ready to use, unlike the chargers, I didn't mention the AUX to the passenger at the beginning of the trip. In this case, I believe it made them feel happier when they asked for it and they received it. Just as a surprise!

And...

Unfortunately, it is very important to have a few brand new and thick plastic bags in the car. Guess why?

To Riders and Readers:

Please be kind to Rideshare drivers!!

When you are doing just a ride, they are doing their job, making their living and their family's livelihood depends on that job.

If you are a rider, paying drivers unfairly and poorly rates puts their financial lives at risk. If you are driving, honking is only accepted to avoid an accident and it is not an act to express anger at the other driver's mistake. Especially if that driver is a rideshare, please be kinder. Your continuous beeping affects that rideshare driver's rate.

This job is hard enough for drivers, please don't make it harder.

This is not easy money to make at all. If you are going into this job with the mindset of making easy money, please be aware that you are doing yourself a serious financial disservice while making the profession more difficult for other drivers.

If you don't have a good car which is fuel efficient (consumes less than 20% of your income to buy gas), **if** you can't manage to deal with an unbelievable tax figure at the end of the year, **if** you can't bear to face the back-breaking cost of car repairs, and **If** you don't know how to handle rude passengers, this is not the right career for you.

Please be kinder to rideshare drivers.

CHAPTER 18

Short stories

CHAPTER 18.1

Oh father!

Among the many trips I made, sometimes passengers asked me for very strange things! Items ranged from common things such as water, chargers, candy, chewing gum to more weird items like pain killers, headache pills, hand lotions, tuna sandwiches and even dental floss!

One day, I had a sore throat, so I bought a package of cough drops, but I searched and found out that the ingredients might lead to a DUI if the police pulled me over, so I stopped using them and put them in my car's console. Over time, whenever someone coughed, I would offer the cough drops, and it netted me about $200 in tips while I was offering it for free only to help the riders!

* * *

My funniest memory of the strange things that some riders asked me was from the night that I had two passengers, a man and a woman. It was clear that they have known each other for a long time. When they came to the car, the man immediately asked me, *"Hey, buddy, do you have an extra condom in your car by any chance?"* I was just shocked!

He: I need a condom. Do you know what that is? Me: Excuuuse me?!!! For here or to go?!

He: Ahhh, I NEED it! Me: Okay, I will stop somewhere to buy it!

Condom logo: Oh father!

CHAPTER18.2

Shameless Proposals

I read an interesting article about ride sharing and sexual harassment. In the introduction, the author mentioned that one out of three women is being exposed to some kind of sexual harassment during her lifetime, but women aren't the only ones with this problem. Men can be exposed to sexual harassment as well!

The article said that, like anywhere else, this problem may occur during a rideshare trip. Rider and driver may be exposed to sexual harassment. That article suggested different ways to protect a person against sexual harassment. To me, one of those ways was very funny. It said don't get involved in any conversation that may lead to this issue. Instead, pretend not to understand the offer!

You can politely skip the issue if you look like someone who doesn't understand the topic and the offer at all!

I can't give you any advice because I am not an expert. I can share my experience, and I believe ignorance or pretending to not getting the offer works. It has really protected me. Thank God, I haven't had any problems about this issue because of a funny reason! I cannot recognize that it's an offer right at the moment they offer it! Fortunately, I may later understand the meaning of those particular conversations when it's too late! I guess I am not smart enough in this kind of situation! HaHaHa this is a sad-fortunate situation!

Girl: You smell good!

Girl: I want to give you a kiss as a tip!!

Me: I'm a little short on my rent, I wish you could come and kiss my landlord!

* * *

Boy: Dude, do you ever hook up between your trips? Me: Hookah? [That's what I heard, "hookah"]

Me: No, it's not allowed because I may get a DUI!

***

Girl: Is it your last ride tonight? This complex has many overnight guest parking spots!

Me: Wow, that's perfect for increasing the value of your apartment!

Unfortunately, this time was the only time that I immediately got what was the issue! You know what? I don't want to talk about it! Let's talk about something else!

* * *

Tip

When you're working, just work! This is one of the most important secrets of being professional and successful!

CHAPTER 18.3

Did You Forget Something?

While working as a rideshare driver, I found so many different items that people left in my car. I reported all of them to the companies, and I tried to find the owners. Some of those items were so strange that I wrote them in my notes and took pictures of them as well. Some very unusual items like brass knuckles, a hundred-dollar bill, a few boxes of baked octopus, a tiny pack that looked like crystal meth and women's underwear! One of those items was just the best, ever!

If someone tells you, "Half a goot nife," immediately check the back seat because he has left his dentures!

Hafe a goot nife!

Vasna Nozari

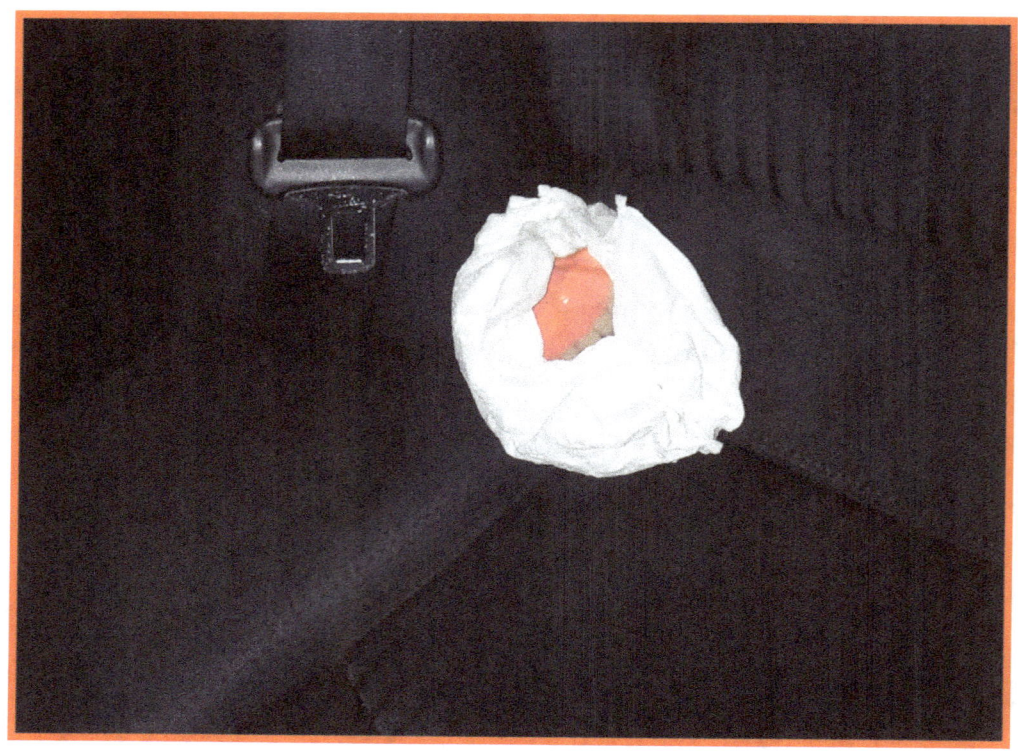

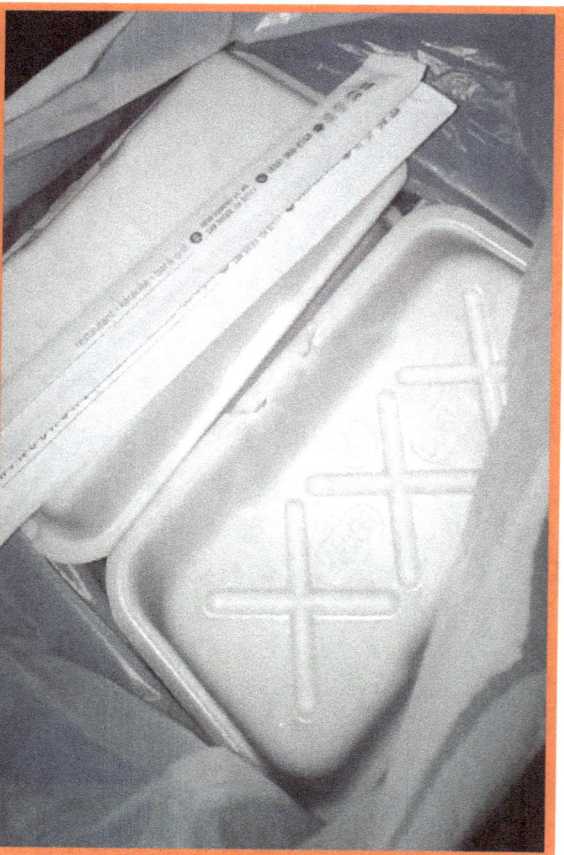

I don't eat octopus. The owner told me to donate it!

Donating octopus at 4 a.m.? It was one of the most difficult tasks that I have ever done!

Tip

Reporting the lost items that you find is very important and it add to your professional credit. Also, in most cases you will receive a bonus for returning the item.

CHAPTER 18.4

On Valentine's Day

Excellent Service

"You're a gentleman, a safe driver and very hospitable Ted there should be more drivers like you it was very nice to lucky enough to have you as a driver"

★★★★★

I got this review on Valentine's Day I really like it but, Ted!?   What do you mean!?

CHAPTER 18.5

Halloween

I remember years ago, an anthropology professor told me, *"You learn a lot about people by watching their celebrations."*

One of the coolest experiences I had in this job was from working on Halloween. I saw three memorable costumes that night.

First, I had a middle-aged man with two green ears on his head and a green tail hanging from the back of his jacket by a binder clip. His tail got stuck in the car door, and out it came!

Me: Sir, Sir! Your tail was cut off!

Me: Don't forget your tail!

* * *

I had a lot of passengers that night, but the second passenger with a very memorable costume was Jerry. At the pick-up point, I looked for him and saw a man standing across the street, so I thought he was Jerry. I drove toward that man while a woman in a bathrobe and high heels and heavy makeup walked after the car as fast as she could. Suddenly, he broke one of his heels and fell!

The reason that I changed the pronoun from "she" to "he" was not a grammar mistake. Jerry's bathrobe opened as he fell!

Jerry: Wait waiiiiiiit!!

Jerry: It is Halloween! Me: I said nothing, sir!

* * *

Late that night, I had a passenger who I took far out of the city, where even the roads were not paved. On the way back, I lost my navigation signal and lost my way. After driving half a mile, I saw a house, so I went to ask for the address. I saw a creature in front of that house. Something about 7 feet tall, in a black cloth with two bright red eyes and legs that looked like horse's hoofs! It freaked me out that bad that I turned around quickly, screamed loudly, and kept repeating to myself, *"Calm down, don't be scared, it is Halloween. Oh f*** it is Halloween!"*

After that ride, I went home to change my pants!

Tip 💡

You don't want to lose the network here on a Halloween night! Be smart when you choose a cellphone company!

CHAPTER 19

Let's Have Peace

One of my most lovely memories in this job was from two Canadian passengers.

I believe Canadians are among the nicest and most peaceful people in the world. They are polite and honorable.

That night was one of the coldest nights in San Diego, something around 45 degrees Fahrenheit. I picked up a Canadian passenger named Nathan. I told him:

Me: Sir, is the temperature fine here inside the car? I know it's too cold outside so please let me know if you need it warmer.

Nathan: Thank you for asking. The temperature is perfect, even outside! Wow, I love it! I'm Canadian, so if this is your coldest weather here, I will gladly deal with it!

Me: Hahaha. Are you here for a conference?

Nathan: No, a little vacation. Are you Iraqi?

Me: No, why do you ask?

Nathan: I traveled here to attend the wedding of my Iraqi friend. It was last night. You look a bit like one of the guests in that party.

Me: Hahaha. No, that wasn't me. How was the party?

Nathan: Oh God, that was the best wedding party ever in my life! I enjoyed every minute of that. Very interesting and funny!

Me: Hahaha. I know exactly how fun it is. I'm Persian and I was at one of my Iraqi friend's wedding two months ago. They are very cool people, and the way they celebrate is super fun.

Nathan: Wow, that's very nice. You are Persian, and you have Iraqi friends. I was thinking you guys may have a problem with each other.

Me: Why? Because of that war?

Nathan: Yes.

Me: Iraqi people have a great historical civilization and culture as we have. All over the world, it is not the people who choose to fight. It's the governments. The people are the innocent victims, they get involved in war without any options. People like weddings, not war!

* * *

A few weeks later, I got another Canadian passenger. He was a little drunk, but a polite and talkative gentleman named Felix.

The destination was 50 miles away from the pick-up point in one of the Navy bases. Although it was cold, I offered him a bottle of cold water, and he drank it with pleasure. He said six months ago he was in the Middle East, so we started talking about that region.

Felix: Man, I really enjoy this conversation. You are a very nice person, and you know a lot about the Middle East. It's been a few months. You are the very first person who knows what's going on out there.

Me: Haha. Maybe they know, but they are not as bad a blabber as I am!

Felix: Hahaha!

Me: Is the location that we are going to, a military base?

Felix: Yes, it is. I'm a pilot of an F-18 fighter serving in the international forces of the Canadian Air Force. I'm here for a joint military exercise with U.S. forces.

Me: F-18 ...

Felix: Yes, sir, Haha. Where are you coming from?

Me: I'm Persian.

Felix: Wow, next month we are probably going to the Persian Gulf.

Me: Ooh!!!

There was a heavy silence for a few moments and then he said:

Felix: We're going there only for a joint maneuver drill.

Me: Have you ever been in a war?

[Another heavy silence.]

Felix: Two times.

Me: [silence]

Felix: But I have never bombed civilians…I mean…They were ISIS…

Me: [silence]

Felix: They were bad people…

Me: You don't need to explain it to me, sir. I didn't say anything.

[More heavy silence.]

Felix: They were bad people …

Me: [silence]

Felix: …One time … in Libya … They were the police and the bodyguards of that dictator …

Me: Sir … Sir…

Felix: … not civilian…

He did not seem to hear me. It was as if he was defending himself as he sat in judgment of himself.

Me: Sir…

Felix: Yes.

Me: Sir, nobody blames you for serving your country or the international forces.

Felix: I know, but you are a good man. I just want you to know that I'm also a good and fair person.

Me: I know, and this is very sad that we both are good!

Felix: What do you mean?

Me: Next month is my sister's wedding. Imagine me going over there for the wedding ceremony, and at the same time you go to that region for the maneuver. If a war happens, according to the law in my country, when there's a war, I no longer have the right to leave the country and I am obligated to be sent to war. I am an artist who has never touched a weapon. My family is behind me, and you are in the front! What should I do? What should we both do? War is not a solution.

He didn't say anything, his eyes were glassy…a good man, a fighter! People should have another option…

People like weddings not war!

CHAPTER 20

Nations

According to the statistics from one rideshare company, in the first six months that I drove, I met, and I gave rides to passengers from more than 30 different countries in the world!

I found this statistic so interesting. It made me think that I should take advantage of this opportunity. So, after that, I decided that whenever I had a passenger from a different country, I should ask them to talk about interesting things in their culture that could be either a tradition or an art. I asked all those passengers to name a favorite food from their country as well, so later I could research about that culture and maybe try that food if I could find it.

Almost a year later, I had met and driven people from several dozen countries. If I had enough time to talk to a person, and if that conversation was interesting, it made me write about that country. I wish I had the opportunity to write about many of my other favorite countries in this book, such as France, Germany, Italy, Austria, Switzerland, Greece, but I didn't have the opportunity to have an interesting conversation with the riders of many of those nations, so you only see the most interesting experiences that I had with the riders from a few nations.

CHAPTER 20.1

Japan

The first country that I want to mention is Japan, the Land of the Rising Sun, and cherry blossoms.

One day when I was coming back from shooting a property, my app was on, and I got a trip request from a car repair shop. I went to the pick-up point and my passenger was an old Japanese gentleman whose name I thought was Ken. He needed to leave his car in the repair shop, so I gave him a ride back to his home, which was far out of the city. We traveled uphill along a narrow, winding road.

I really wanted to start a conversation with him, but he was looking at the rocks silently, as if he was doing some kind of meditation.

After a few minutes, I spoke to him very slowly.

Me: Sir ...

Me: Ken...Ken? I have a bottle of cold water here if you like...

Man: Akira. Ken is that repairman...How do you like this car?

Me: I'm so happy with it. Are you originally Japanese? I appreciate this good car…

Akira: This is why I don't want to replace my car. I learned to repair the thing, but people here don't repair, they just suggest replacing everything!

We should respect and appreciate our relationship with those around us!

Me: I have a bottle of cold water here if you like to have it. I like your name Akira. One of my favorite filmmakers has the same name.

Akira: Kurosawa?

Me: Yes sir.

Akira: Is this water for free?

Me: Sure, it is.

Akira: Thank you, thank you.

Akira: You like watching films?

Me: I love it. Do you like …?

Akira: I haven't watched TV for 35 years!

Me: Really? But what about your family?

Akira: I live here alone.

Me: How can you not be bored?

Akira: I have many old thick books with pictures and paintings. You can watch a picture for hours like a Kamishibai. You need to read and think, then you can write!

Me: What is kami…?

When he explained Kamishibai to me, I remembered that I had read about it in a theater history book. I recalled exactly what he was talking about because there was a similar style of theatre in my culture as well.

I searched Kamishibai and according to Wikipedia, it means "paper play" and it is a form of Japanese street theater and storytelling that was popular during the Depression of the 1930s and the post-war period in Japan until the invention of television during the 20th century.

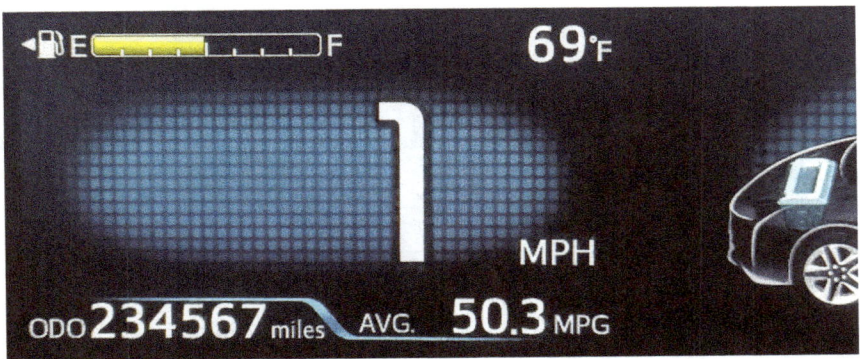

Although he was not that talkative, I really enjoyed talking with him, and at the end of the trip he surprised me with a good tip. He was a kind and generous person, and I am very happy that I was able to start a conversation with him. He also said his favorite food is Karē raisu, which is a kind of steamed rice with curry stew.

Japanese food: Scan the first QR code to access the food gallery. Scan the other codes for more!

CHAPTER 20.2

China

One day, I had a passenger who had written her name in a form that looked like what is used in China or other Asian countries. I went to the pick-up point, which was a crowded terminal, and there were a few Asian men and women. No one came to my car to get in, so I called the account holder's number through the app. Unfortunately, it went to voicemail.

I didn't want to cancel the trip, so I got out of my car. I could not read that name in that Asian script, so I had to show my phone to each of the people that I guessed could be my passenger; I asked, "Is this you?" OMG!

Finally, I showed that to a lady, and she exploded with laugher! We got in the car, and she told me her name was Lan.

Lan: Sorry, my phone died, and I was a little confused. Thank God, you found me.

Me: Ma'am, I couldn't even read your name to call it. Why did you write your name in the Chinese alphabet?

Lan: I am an elementary school teacher...because of the training rule that we use for the kids, I was following the same rule which I ask my students to follow, so we wrote everything just in our language to follow the rules. I wrote my name like that. I forgot to change it later.

Me: Lan? Your name shouldn't have three letters?

Lan: That's not a letter, that is a character, and somehow it is a symbol or a shape which belongs to a word.

Me: Really!? How many of those are in your language?

Lan: Around 50,000.

Me: Oh my God! Are you saying that every person has to memorize fifty thousand characters to be able to read and write?

Lan: No, around two thousand is enough for daily needs and ten thousand for the university level.

Me: Wow, you guys are smart! There is no way that I can do this, but I would be happy if I could just write the name of my love.

Lan: What is her name?

Me: His name is Mr. Wu!

Lan: Is he a man?

Me: He is an adult panda who lives in the San Diego Zoo, but he will be sent to Beijing soon. We all love him, from here to Beijing.

Lan: Hahaha. Those lovely animals are ambassadors of peace between the nations.

* * *

I asked her what her favorite Chinese dish was, and she said hot pot.

Chinese food_ Scan the first QR code to access the food gallery. Scan the other codes for more!

CHAPTER 20.3

India

I have had a lot of Indian passengers. Having Indian passengers somehow is fun because most of them are smart, nice, and love music. I remember one day, I had a newly married Indian couple as my passengers. They asked if they could use an AUX cable. I told them they sure could. They played their music and even started to dance. I thought those kinds of scenes just happen in their movies! They performed it live in my car, and it was really a good memory. At the end of the music, they got very emotional. The man put his wife on his lap, and they began to sing. It was a great example of Indian romance, and it reminded me of another great story of Indian romance, why the Taj Mahal ("Crown Palace") was built.

Empress Mumtaz Mahal, born into a family of Persian nobility, was the Emperor Shah Jahan's beloved wife, but she died giving birth to their 14th child, and this plunged the emperor into a great sorrow. It is said that his hair quickly turned gray after his beloved wife died in his arms. According to the United Nations Educational, Scientific and Cultural Organization (UNESCO) world heritage center's website, Shah Jahan built an immense mausoleum of white marble in Agra between 1631 and 1648, in memory of his favorite wife. The Taj Mahal is the jewel of art in India and one of the universally admired masterpieces of the world. Taj Mahal is a symbol of India's rich history.

I had another Indian passenger in my car, and that guy was super funny. I gave him a cold bottle of water, mint candy, and a phone charger. We really enjoyed talking to each other. He introduced a few Indian dishes to me such as: biryani, dosa, aloo paratha. His name was something like Baja, if I remember it correctly.

We were laughing and he told me:

Baja: Okay, my friend, this was a really good trip, so I am going to give you a great tip! Hahaha!

Me: Hahaha! I enjoyed talking to you, tipping is not necessary.

Baja: No, no, no, I must do it, and this is magical money! Hahaha!

Me: Oh really? Haha…

Baja: Believe me, this is very special money! You can build your dream with this. Do you have a dream?

Me: Yes, I want to build a new center, a new home, for some kids. Are you going to pay for that?

Baja: Sure! Here you are!

He gave me a dollar tip. We both laughed so much that tears came to our eyes. He told me, *"This is a magic one, believe me, look at that!"* The money had funny writing on top (see the picture below). He looked like a student, so I felt I needed to appreciate his good attitude. I gladly accepted that dollar bill. I told him: *"I'm going to write about this in my book. Okay? And one day I will put this money in a magic frame, and I will sell that frame for the children!"*

Indian food – Scan the first QR code to access the food gallery. Scan the other codes for more!

CHAPTER 20.4

Mexico

I had a lot of Mexican-American passengers. In a city like San Diego, which shares a border with Mexico, it is very normal to have Mexican-American passengers. It is very easy to get to know them better and get acquainted with their culture.

They are kind, hardworking, and sociable people who will be very good friends if they want to become friends with you.

One late night, I picked up two men and a woman from the front of a large villa. They were dressed up like a mariachi* music group.

---

*   *Mariachi: Mariachi is a genre of regional Mexican music that dates back to at least the 18th century. The usual mariachi group today consists of three to eight artists who play traditional Mexican music.*

They carried a lot of things including a mini luggage and a big guitar, which I put in the trunk, and an instrument that maybe was a vihuela, a five-string guitar-like instrument. The man in the front seat kept it on his lap because it didn't have a case or cover.

The lady had a big container of food, which later on I found out had tacos inside. She also had two instruments. When they started playing, I heard something that sounded like "Castanets**", but I couldn't see them!

The other man had a trumpet-like instrument that I had never seen before, and in the other hand he had a bottle of tequila!

The funniest thing was they couldn't speak English at all. Not even one sentence!

They were going to the Tijuana border, which was around 35 miles from the pick-up point.

The man in the front seat showed my profile picture on his phone to make sure that they were in the right car. I confirmed, then I pointed to the bottle of tequila and said to the man in the back seat," Sir, let me put the bottle in the trunk. If it is an open container, we are not allowed to keep it here." He said, "No, no, no" and hid the bottle under his clothes. I told him: "Sir it's not open, correct?" They looked at each other a little confused, spoke a few sentences in their own language and then the guy on the backseat nodded like a positive sign and said, "Ojala!"

I started the trip, then asked the man in front, "Are you going to the main border station?" They looked to each other again, then started to laugh, and all three told me, "Ojala! Ojala!"

After two minutes I pointed to the cold-water bottles and told them, "Water, anybody…? Cold water?"

The lady happily took a bottle and drank it. I pointed to another bottle of water and said to the man in front: "Water?" He turned his head toward the other man and with a laugh said, "Tequila?"

I said, "Oh God! No, no, no tequila here!" They laughed, and I knew they were kidding, so I started laughing as well. The front-seat guy looked at me again and asked, "No tequila?"

 I smiled and said, "You cannot drink tequila in the car. No, no tequila, Señor!" He sighed and said, "Taco?"

I didn't get what he meant by saying taco. They laughed and kept saying "Taco, taco." I don't know why, but I said "Ojala!" Their laughter intensified, and while all three were saying "Ojala," the lady opened the container and gave each man a taco, then with motherly kindness brought a taco near my face! I looked at them with rounded eyes. It was too late to say that they cannot eat in the car! I told her, "I'm driving, Ma'am!" She kept repeating "Taco, taco," so I gave her a paper towel and she wrapped that taco for me.

** For more information and see related video, please scan the QR codes at the end of this chapter.

That was the time that I saw the woman had many tacos in the container, which probably was from the party. They ate one or two more tacos, and that kind woman wrapped a second taco for me in a paper towel.

After they ate, the front man asked me again,

"No tequila? Hahaha!" And the other man said: *"Ojala?"*

We laughed loudly. I told them, *"No Ojala! No!"*

Then he said, *"Music Ojala?"*

This time, I knew what would happen if I said "Ojala!" I said "Ojala," and for more than 10 minutes they played great music and sang. It was an unforgettable memory, and my first mariachi experience from that close!

At the destination, when they left the car, I immediately parked somewhere and searched for the meaning of the word Ojala.

The result that I found warmed my heart. "Ojala" in Spanish means "God willing," and that word comes from the Arabic "In sha'Allah" meaning "God willing." When I found it, I remembered that although they were talking in Spanish, I recognized the word "Arab." Then they said, "Ojala." I guess maybe they thought I was Arabic, so they tried to touch my heart and communicate with the only common word they knew.

There was a language barrier between us, but they climbed that wall and kindly shared whatever they could with me, their food, their music, and their happiness.

It warmed my heart!

Mexican food – Scan the first QR code to access the food gallery. Scan the other codes for more!

CHAPTER 20.5

Turkey

"The wound is the place where the Light enters you."
- Rumi

Rumi is my absolutely favorite poet, and this is one of the most beautiful quotes attributed* to him that I preferred to start my story with, however the story is about another poem and other quotes!

Mawlānā Jalāl ad-Dīn Muhammad Balkhī better known as Rūmī, was a Persian poet, mystic and leader of the Sufis. When the Mongols invaded Central Asia, he with his family and a group of disciples, set out westwards. This was also the beginning of a spiritual journey, and his words and popularity went far beyond the borders of Iran. His burial shrine is in Konya, Turkey. There are many followers who every year do a super interesting spiritual whirling and Sufi dance known as Sama.

Many people consider Rumi's thoughts a spiritual link between nations. Rumi said, "Empathy is even better than talking in one language."

---

*   *Interpretation of American poet Coleman Barks from a poem by Rumi.*

One day, I really felt this quote. I had a passenger from Turkey who could barely speak English. I picked him up from the airport and saw a sticker from Istanbul Airport on his luggage.

He took the front seat and looked so tired. The weather was hot, so I offered him a bottle of cold water. I told him to feel free to adjust the AC temperature, so he felt more comfortable. He turned the AC off and didn't even look at the water that I offered!

I immediately realized that I should drive the 46 miles with my mouth shut! I was not worried about my rating. Instead, I was a little worried about a traditional rough teaching system that his generation would use to teach a lesson about the benefits of being quiet and polite!

His name was Aziz, after 10 minutes of silence Aziz said:

Aziz: Twenty-three-hour flight. Tired!

Me: Oh my God, I know exactly how exhausted you are. I was in Istanbul last year. When I arrived here, I slept for 14 hours.

Aziz: Why you go there? [He meant why I was there]

Me: I went there to see some places in Konya, then I went to Istanbul from there.

[He got excited, took one of the waters, opened it, and drank a little.]

Aziz: My city, Konya.

Me: That's a beautiful city.

Aziz: Beautiful, Very Beeeeautiful.

[It seemed Aziz had forgotten he was tired as he found a common feeling with a person after many hours of loneliness.

Again, he barely could speak English, I can't speak Turkish and he couldn't speak Farsi, but we talked for 35 minutes about all the enjoyable common things in our culture. About Rumi, about Sama, about beautiful Konya, about Aziz Nesin, my favorite Turkish writer, about the delicious baklava pastry and the common food that both cultures have.

"Empathy is even better than talking in one language."

Turkish food – Scan the first QR code to access the food gallery. Scan the other codes for more!

CHAPTER 20.6

United Kingdom

One day, I had a British gentleman as my passenger. If you ask me how I distinguish a British passenger from others, I should say it is not that difficult.

He got into the back seat, I asked his name, and he told me it was Archie, which is a common name in the UK. After starting the trip, I offered him a bottle of cold water. He said:

Archie: Oh water, yes please, it is too hot here.

Me: Actually, it's not that hot today. Maybe you've compared it to London.

As I always do, I gave the bottle to him with a napkin because it's fancier and the passenger's hand does not get wet. He looked at the napkin. He looked to the napkin and said:

Archie: Huh, interesting! Do you also have something for rubbish?

Me: Yes sir, give it to me, I have a plastic bag under my seat for trash.

Archie: Huh, interesting! And why did you mention London?

Me: I guess you might be British.

Archie: Yes, I am, but how did you find out?

Me: I had a few British passengers before. I can recognize a British passenger from three things. First, from the arrogant tone and the way you're pronouncing words and placing stress. I noticed in some words that end in the letter "R," you guys pronounce it "ah."

Sir, you said, "wotah" instead of "water."

Second, British people use some word which is not common among American, like the word "rubbish" that you used instead of "trash."

Archie: Alright, very interesting! How do you know it?

Me: I knew just a little English before coming to the U.S., and the books that are being used there are mostly British English, so when I came here for a while, I had some funny problems.

Archie: Haha, like what?

Me: The very first day in the airport I badly needed to use the restroom and the only thing that I knew for it, was "WC," which is an abbreviation for "water closet" and it's not that common in the U.S. I didn't know the word restroom, so the first five people that I asked them, "Where is WC?" couldn't figure out what I was talking about. As a result, for ten minutes I was running around with a red face and looking for WC and …

Archie: Hahaha, I had a similar problem. Americans say eraser and we say rubber, but here rubber means something else! For a few days in the office, I asked one of my female colleagues to lend me her rubber!

Me: Hahahaha!

Archie: What is the third way to identify a British passenger?

Me: I notice that after finishing the trip, especially when British passengers are happy with the service, they knock the car!

Archie: What?

Me: Believe it or not, all my British passengers and a few old American passengers unconsciously did it. Mostly, they knocked on the roof of the car after disembarking. For a while, I was really confused and even pissed off about why they do this and why mostly the British do it. I searched about it, and I found something…In the Victorian era, passengers would hit the roof of a carriage to make the driver stop, then they give the fare right there on top of the roof, and if they were happy with the ride, they would knock again and give another coin as tips.

Archie: Haha makes sense.

He left the car and said, *"I enjoyed this ride and conversation."* Then…

Knock Knock!

British food – Scan the first QR code to access the food gallery. Scan the other codes for more!

He told me that the British love potatoes. Would you like the British people to love you?

Tip

Keep the water cold and fancy, then make money off it!

CHAPTER 20.7

Saudi Arabia

One day I had a passenger who asked me a very interesting question. She was a polite lady who would consider her ethnic group "White, not Hispanic." Her name was Anna.

She asked me, "Do you feel angry if I ask you where you are from?" Actually, that was a very shocking and interesting question, especially since she asked it without any warm-up or introduction.

Before I could answer, Anna said that the last driver got very upset when she very politely asked him the same question.

She told me that the driver reacted angrily and said, *"Should I answer your question?"*

I thought for a moment…

Me: Ma'am did you rate him bad?

Anna: Honestly, yes, because his answer hurt my feelings.

Me: I can guess why he got upset.

Anna: why?

Me: Ma'am I am Persian, and I am proud of it. I don't know where he was from, but maybe he was afraid that his answer causes a negative prejudgment in your mind. Maybe he was worried about his stars rate which can affect his financial life*. You may not like an answer and rate him badly as you did!

Anna: But …

Me: I know, he did not give you a nice answer, but maybe he was tired of the question which put him down, just because of prejudgment. We are all human beings, and we live with each other. These groupings, separate human beings, cause stereotyping, prejudice, and conflict.

Anna: I like your answer, but I still cannot understand that much anger.

Me: Okay, let me ask you a question. Your name is Anna, it may come from Anne, who was the mother of the Virgin Mary. In Turkey, Anna is used as a word which means mother. They are mostly Muslims! However, the origin of your name probably comes from a Hebrew name Hannah which means "grace." So, how would you feel if I looked at your name suspiciously, then turned my head and asked you: "Are you Jewish?" or "Are you Christian or even Muslim?"

Anna: I will remember it, thanks!

* * *

The very same day, in a big hotel in San Diego, an educational conference was being held for young Arab people, mostly from Saudi Arabia and United Arab Emirates. I had a passenger from that conference whose name was Fahad, which is a common family name in that country, so when I saw that, I immediately recognized he could be from Saudi Arabia.

Iran and Saudi Arabia are in the same region. In that region, people of those countries live near each other, but they haven't felt good about each other in a long time. Maybe it's just because of misunderstandings, prejudices, and unnecessary conflicts. I remember, at that time, there was a bad conflict between Iran and Saudi Arabia which could even lead to a war, and it is more serious than being worried about a rating!

Although, I offered him a bottle of cold water and I did my normal respectful service, I didn't want him to find out that I'm Persian, so I hoped he wouldn't ask where I'm from. He did!

He started the conversation like this:

Fahad: Oh, my friend, this phone charger here is very helpful, and thank you for water. You are a good man. Where are you from?

Me: I'm Persian.

Fahad: Oh! Iran?

---

*   *To find out how rate may affect the financial life please read chapter 17.*

Me: Hahaha yes, why did you say, "Oh?"

Fahad: Nothing, you are a good one!

Me: Haha, if you don't mind, let me ask you something.

Fahad: Sure.

Me: You said I'm a good one! Have you had an experience with a bad Persian personally?

Fahad: Hmmm …myself…no, I didn't, but you probably know overall how we think about each other?

Me: Yes, with negative mentality and prejudice, we look to stereotype and judge each other.

Fahad: Exactly, and I really hate when other people look at me with those mindsets and stereotypes, no matter where and which country… Two days ago, I was in an airport outside of the U.S. One of that airport's security guards was arguing with me over my luggage. He was thinking that I am very rich, and I have an oil well in my backyard. Maybe he was thinking that I don't know anything about airport rules, so he can charge me more! I'm an engineer and an artist. I work for my expenses…I was coming from one of the best and biggest airports ever in the world, which was in my country. He made me feel very upset and angry.

Me: Yes, I know exactly that feeling. That's sad and we have to end it. First, we need to stop the stereotyping ourselves. I like art as well. Let's talk about art.

He told super interesting information about Al-Hamra'a Museum in one of the world's largest open-air art galleries in Jeddah. Then we talked about sports and our favorite soccer clubs, which both wear blue shirts, and they would play each other very soon in the AFC Cup.

We only talked about art and sports, and at the destination we were like two close friends. He shook my hand, and I told him I really enjoyed talking to him. People just needed to find a reason to let the bad feelings go away!

Saudi Arabian food – Scan the first QR code to access the food gallery. Scan the other codes for more!

CHAPTER 20.8

Iran

I'm Persian, and this story is about one of the few times that I had a Persian passenger. I mean, I "kind of" had a Persian passenger. It's weird and funny and I will explain what I mean, but before I start, I would like to state some facts about Persians.

First, Persians are proud. Actually, one of the reasons that most of us like to call ourselves Persian instead of Iranian is that we like to be proud of the ancient Persian Empire. In fact, we cannot live without being proud of something! Please don't misunderstand, we are a nice and humble people. We are not narcissistic, we just need to be proud, and we are addicted to being proud. It's like a drug and a chemical process in our bodies!

The range of what we can be proud of could be as wide as the first human rights declaration in history (by Cyrus the Great) to the point that we are proud to wash our butt! Oh yes, we wash it, you don't?! Oh dude!

Smile, don't get angry. I know sometimes we act with too much pride, but just let us be proud. Then you will see how cool, calm, and nice we will become. We'll be like a fluffy Persian cat that sometimes gets on your nerves, then he calms down, and you really enjoy keeping him in your life. Of course, in the case of the Persian people there are many good reasons, other than enjoying their company.

Believe it or not, I do not say it because I am Persian. I strongly believe every person should have a Persian friend, and every group should have a Persian member because we always find a solution. A funny, easy and f***** smart solution! This is the second fact about Persian!

Before telling the third fact, let me tell the story of my Persian passenger.

One night around 3 a.m., I got a call, and the pick-up point was in front of a 7-Eleven store. That night was one of the most important Persian celebrations, which is called "Yalda Night*" and it is the longest and darkest night of the year.

After that night, daylight hours increase every day, as if the light was born at the end of that night and started to grow. The word "Yalda" also means birthday. Persians celebrates the birth of light the same week as the Christmas celebration. A birthday for light from 502 BC.

That night, Persian families would gather together and celebrate as late as they can even until sunrise! They put a lot of fruit, nuts, and other snacks on a large table, and sometimes spend the whole night playing music, reading poetry, storytelling, and having fun.

When I arrived at the parking lot of that 7-Eleven, my phone started ringing, and it was my passenger. His name on the app was Mo, which probably was a short form of his real name and was why I did not recognize he was Persian.

I answered the phone.

Mo: Hi, buddy, this is Mo, the rider of this ride.

Me: Hello, sir. Are you here, I'm in front of 7-Eleven, I cannot see you…

Mo: Because I'm not there, and this is why I called you.

Me: Oh, okay. Should I pick up someone else?

Mo: Actually no, but may I ask you to do me a favor?

Me: Sure, if I can.

Mo: May I ask you to tap to start the trip, then go to the store, buy me a cigarette, and then drive to the destination which is my house? I'm waiting here for you. I will pay the price of cigarettes plus very good tips to you.

Me: Ay, baba! [I whispered it in my language, it means: Oh father! or Oh Lord and we (Persian) say it when we are surprised or displeased]…

Mo: …Hahaha! Are you Persian? I knew it, I could guess it by your name and accent; "Begir bia Baba." [It means: Take it and bring, my son.]

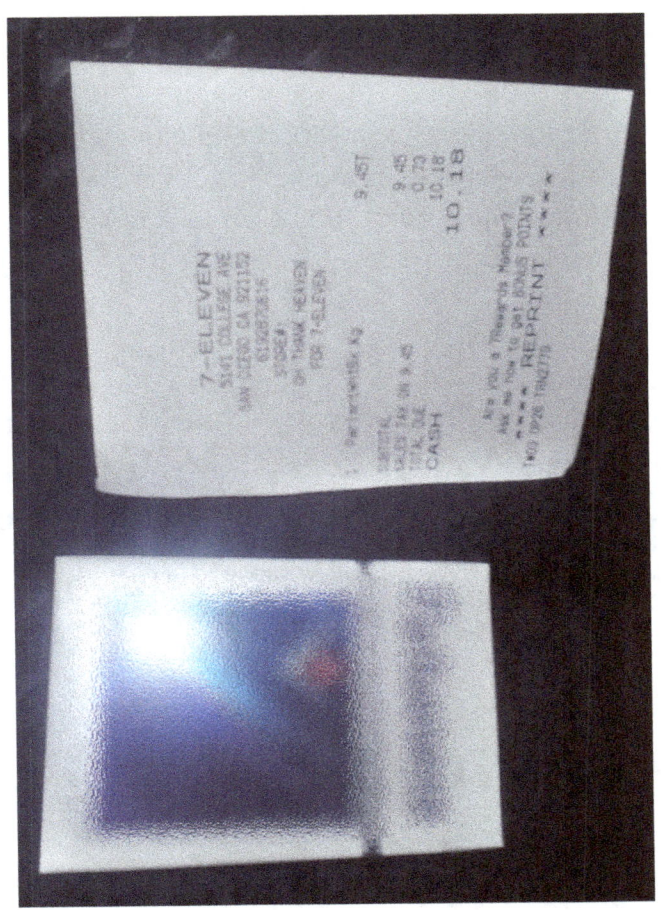

When I got to his house, he came out with a bunch of nuts, fruits, and food and before I could talk, he asked me a question.

Mo: Did you have a good celebration tonight?

Me: No, I'm working on a goal.

Mo: Oh my God! Leave the goals for another night! Family and traditions come first, son.

Me: Okay!

Mo: Come onnnn! Take these nuts and fruit and eat them all before morning!

Me: Okay!

Mo: I'm sorry, this was a long night, and I ran out of cigarettes. Listen to me, my son, don't smoke ever. Cigarettes are a monster that make you addicted.

Me: Oh God!

Mo: Yeah… a monster…! Okay, son, this is your money and tip, I wish you could come in and celebrate with us. Don't forget family comes first!

A final fact I want to share about Persian people is we love to share our experiences. You see...we can even write a book about it!

While he was giving me some more pieces of advice, I remembered the face of Eihab, when I told him to spray cologne in his car! Whatever goes around, comes around! But I also felt proud of what I shared because I did it with my whole heart. However, as a punishment and to be polite I kept listening to Mo's advice for 20 minutes!

A week later, at midnight, I had a passenger in his pajamas going to a store to buy cigarettes. He asked me to wait for him, then give him a ride back to his home. On our way to his home, I told him the story of Mo. He said: "Dude that is really the next-level solution!"

Anyway, this book is finished here, but as the last paragraph I need to add something about my pride. The reason that we do that much proud is because we had a lot to be proud of, so we got used to being proud! I mean...Oh some more proud coming, so many more coming...

I am from the oldest country in the world (founded in 3200 BC), the oldest empire in the world, with the most accurate calendar in the world (Jalali calendar). From my homeland comes the basis of much of the world's knowledge such as medicine with Avicenna and mathematics also astronomy with Omar Khayyam and Khwarizmi.

Oooh dear, I feel much better now, and I sincerely appreciate your patience!

Thank you for reading this book.

Take it easy, smile, and take a small step to make others happy :-)

Persian food _ Scan the first QR code to access the food gallery. Scan the other codes for more!

Scan the first QR code to access the book's website, see all galleries, and get more information about traditional ceremonies, places, events, video, music...and to support our charitable goals and to contact us please scan the other QR codes.

www. Dordbook .com

*** This book is dedicated to the **brave women of Iran** who gave a new meaning to the words woman, life and freedom.***

Special thanks to these kind hearts who helped me along my way:

Anthony Keith, Carol Mills, Dr.Jan Jarrell, Gary Holley, Travis Cupples, Dr.Afshin Sepehri, Mehran Sepehri, Majid Nazari, Shahryar Shahryari, Farhad Bahrami, Esmaeil Mihandoust, Afshin Gardouni, Ali Sadr, Bryan Smith, Sahar Hashemi, Borzu Shahryari, Michael Yutan, Jessa Joy, Jessa Amores, Kamran Vali, Sharareh Lotfi, Courtney family, Mosleh family, , ...and

my beloved family.

Thank you very much from the bottom of my heart for all that you did. You are truly appreciated.